Florida's First Big League Baseball Players

Florida's First Big League Baseball Players

A Narrative History

Wes Singletary

THE History PRESS

Published by The History Press
Charleston, SC 29403
www.historypress.net

Cover image: President John F. Kennedy speaks before a capacity crowd at Al Lopez Field, Tampa, Florida, November 1963. *Courtesy Florida State Archives.*
Back cover image: Lopez batting for the Boston Braves. *Courtesy Al Lopez.*

First published 2006
Manufactured in the United States
ISBN 978.1.59629.116.4

Library of Congress Cataloging-in-Publication Data

Singletary, Wes, 1960-
Florida's first big league baseball players : a narrative history /
Wes Singletary.
p. cm.
Includes index.
ISBN 978-1-59629-116-4 (alk. paper)
1. Baseball players--Florida--Biography. I. Title.
GV856.A1S56 2006
796.357092'2--dc22

2006000448

Grateful acknowledgment is made to McFarland Publishing for permission to reprint varied quotations from the book *Al Lopez: The Life of Baseball's El Senor*, 1999.

The stories of Bitsy Mott, Jimmy Bloodworth and Andy Hansen previously appeared in slightly different form in *Nine: A Journal of Baseball History and Social Policy Perspectives*.

For Jimmy Bloodworth, Charlie Cuellar, Al Lopez,
Bitsy Mott, Manuel Onis, Andy Hansen,
Red Barrett and Russ Scarritt

Contents

Preface 9
Acknowledgements 14

Al Lopez 16
Russell Mallory Scarritt 47
Manuel Domingues "Curly" Onis 54
Jimmy Bloodworth 63
Frank "Red" Barrett 72
Andy Hansen 81
Elisha Matthew "Bitsy" Mott 95
Charlie Cuellar 111

Index 121
About the Author 127

Preface

Where do the majority of today's professional baseball players originate? Today, the Latin nations of the Dominican Republic, Puerto Rico, Mexico, Venezuela and even Cuba spring to mind. Historically, though, the states of California, Texas, North Carolina and Alabama produced far more baseball players than might be expected, both for the lily-white "organized" game and its professional Negro League counterpart. While statistics regarding such production remain ambiguous and subject to change, it can be said with relative certainty that certain areas, for whatever reason, produce more baseball players than do others. Florida is such a place.

Dubbed *La Florida* by the Spaniards who first happened upon it during *Pascua Florida*, or the feast of flowers, Florida has become a "feast" of baseball-player development, with many of its native-born diamond hopefuls moving into the professional ranks. In recent years, the state's playgrounds have produced ballplayers in numbers rivaling even those of its prodigious Latin neighbors to the south. The careers of Alex Rodriguez, Johnny Damon, Gary Sheffield, Luis Gonzalez, Carl Everett and Tino Martinez, as well as Lou Piniella, Tony LaRussa, Steve Garvey, Andre Dawson, Hal McRae, Doc Gooden and many others, all dramatically serve to illustrate the case in point. While the reasons for this upturn are numerous—ranging from the warm climate affording year-around participation in the sport to Florida's uniquely diverse and migratory populace—the trend toward mass-produced baseball talent is a relatively recent development.

Perhaps the greatest native-born Florida baseball player was John Henry "Pop" Lloyd, a Hall of Famer and veteran of the Negro Leagues and Cuba who played well

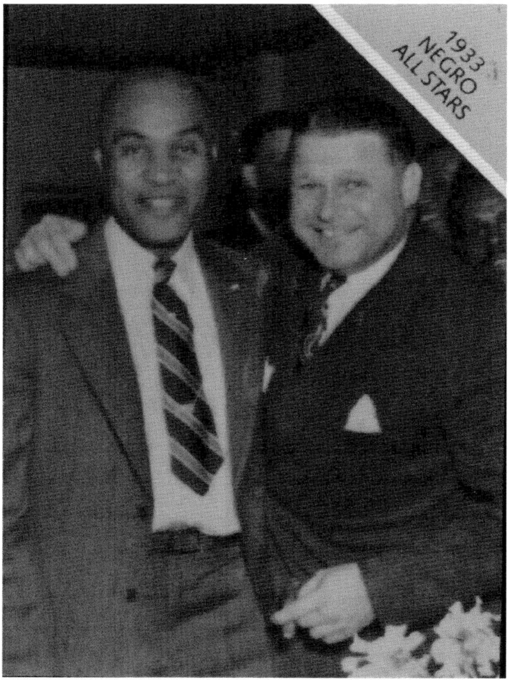

John Henry Lloyd with Jimmy Foxx, 1933. *Courtesy the* Sporting News.

into his fifties. Yet, because organized baseball, through systematic prejudice and willful ignorance, chose to acknowledge a misguided "gentlemen's agreement" rather than sheer ability, this exceptional African American athlete was never afforded the opportunity to compete in the white Major Leagues. Lloyd, often compared in skill to Honus Wagner, the great Hall of Fame Pittsburgh Pirates shortstop, was acknowledged by no less an authority than Babe Ruth as the best baseball player, "organized or unorganized," who ever played the game.

The large majority of native-born Florida players who made it to the Major Leagues prior to 1950—or three years into "Baseball's Great Experiment," the breaking of the color barrier—were scarcely known performers with limited skills, but an abundance of heart. Of course there were the occasional exceptions, such as Tampa's Al Lopez and Lance Richbourg of Defuniak Springs, both of whom enjoyed extended stays in the Majors. However, for most of the others, the proverbial "glass of water" was all they were afforded. These players hailed from the communities of Ybor City, Arcadia, Defuniak Springs, Deland, Lake Worth, Apalachicola, Kissimmee, Yulee, Bartow and Jasper. They also came from the better-known cities of Tampa, Miami, Fort Lauderdale, Pensacola and Jacksonville. Their skills were fashioned in high school and amateur leagues, and are still spoken of locally by old-timers with pride and reverence. Through their efforts, these men helped forge a rich legacy of baseball in a land previously known more for diamondback rattlesnakes than baseball diamonds.

The distinction of having been the first Major League baseball player born in Florida goes to Ralph McLaurin of Kissimmee, who debuted with the St. Louis Cardinals in 1908. McLaurin was in the Majors just long enough to grace a scorecard, going 5 for 22 at the plate over eight games. The 1908 season was not a stellar year for the Cardinals either, as they finished in the cellar with a 49–105 record. Ralph McLaurin died in McColl, South Carolina, in 1943.

Between McLaurin's 1908 appearance and 1950, there were another twenty-five Florida boys that made it to the show. While their names might not strike a familiar chord, they were all once listed on big-league rosters. And as Major Leaguers, they all carved for themselves a slice of "America's game," becoming stitched as part of the national baseball fabric, while harnessing their own unique set of memories to share.

Unfortunately, by the time this project began, all but eight of these Florida baseball pioneers had passed away, taking forever with them tales of life in Florida and the game during this emerging period. In *The Glory of Their Times*, Lawrence Ritter spoke of the urgent need to chronicle the memories of such aging performers before it was too late. He discussed how Ty Cobb's death had inspired Ritter to begin a 75,000-mile journey of dialogue, transcription and reflection. Ritter's effort, which has spawned a myriad of similar works, aptly illustrated that no source could prove better from which to gather information regarding a particular baseball life than the person who lived it. Ritter urged his readers to *listen* to the stories of those he had interviewed. For only by listening to these shared memories could the reader hope to grasp the wealth of experience that was being passed on.

Accepting Ritter's call to urgency, I set upon the journey of locating the eight surviving members of Florida's inaugural baseball fraternity in the hope of capturing all that their collective memories promised. With less effort than one might surmise, I was able to contact and personally interview each of the eight men within a relatively brief two-year period. It proved to be timely, for shortly thereafter a number of these men, Russ Scarritt, Manuel Onis and Charlie Cuellar, died. Within another few years Red Barrett, Bitsy Mott, Andy Hansen and Jimmy Bloodworth followed them. This past autumn saw Al Lopez, then the oldest living Hall of Famer ever, pass at age ninety-seven. This scenario, more than anything else could have, lent credence to Ritter's admonishment to listen while you can, rendering the vivid recollections of these men and the others all the more important.

In preparing the interviews for publication, I, like Ritter, did very little in the way of editing. The questions I asked were eliminated from the transcript so as to provide a flowing narrative of transpired events. This format better illustrates the drama that their stories held. And, from the outset, I believed it was important to conduct each of the interviews in person so as to acquire a better feel for the individual. This I was able to accomplish because of the hospitality shown to me by the former players and their families. It was often a family member who set up the meeting or acted as a memory trigger by posing a question that I had not thought of. In no other interview was this more apparent than when I traveled to Pensacola to speak with the then ninety-one-year-old Russ Scarritt. At the time, Scarritt was convalescing in a nursing home with a broken hip and it was his son, Jerry, who drove me out to the hospital and introduced me to the man who holds the Boston Red Sox record for most triples in a season. Upon arrival I quickly found that while Scarritt had slowed a step or two from his playing days, he still maintained a sharp wit and ready reply. Yet, perhaps because of his age and health, Scarritt was best prodded by his son, who no doubt had heard many of the stories before.

Another example of family hospitality and assistance occurred when I arrived in Tampa to speak with Charlie Cuellar, one of the most prolific minor league pitchers of all time with two hundred-plus victories to his credit. I had hoped to catch up with Cuellar at an annual gathering of former Tampa Smokers, but Cuellar, who had recently been hospitalized suffering kidney problems and a broken arm, was spending the afternoon at home. My visit, at least according to Dahlia Cuellar, Charlie's wife, was designed to take his mind off his ailments, and I admit that it seemed to work. As if on cue, the "Marco Polo of the Minors" was soon alive with tales from his lengthy and colorful career in professional baseball, much to the delight of his wife and guests.

Each visit proved to be an encore of kindness and generosity. I was thrilled when Hall of Famer Al Lopez invited me into his scenic bayside home in Tampa (on what proved to be the first of many such visits) where he was consistently forthright and candid on a number of baseball-related issues. El Señor, then eighty-six years old, looked in excellent condition with a golf game to envy, and I was completely taken with his vitality and strength of character.

Jimmy Bloodworth, the former Washington Senators second baseman, was kind enough to drive from his home in Apalachicola to meet with me and his grandson David over lunch in Tallahassee, and he picked up the tab! A proud grandfather, Jimmy would outlive David, who succumbed to illness a few short years later. I met with Manuel Onis at the Café Creole in Ybor City, Tampa's Latin Quarter. Onis was a vibrant outgoing personality by anyone's account and he spent the luncheon wistfully regaling myself and others with tales of baseball in old Ybor City and his singular opportunity that knocked once.

Both Frank "Red" Barrett and Andy Hansen were kind enough to open their homes to me, and this was deeply appreciated. "Red" Barrett, the pride of St. Leo, was an impressive figure as he greeted me in Leesburg. Retired from a number of business ventures, Barrett and his wife were busy enjoying a quiet life in their central Florida home within close proximity to their grandchildren. Like Barrett, Andy Hansen remained in the type of physical condition that left little wonder that he was once a professional athlete. Hansen, also retired, was living with his recently wedded wife in the beautiful community of Atlantis.

Former Philadelphia Phillies shortstop Bitsy Mott was, without exception, the liveliest and most animated of the group. I had been informed by some of those in Tampa who knew him that this would be the case and Mott did not disappoint. Living on a picturesque hillside in Blue Ridge, Georgia, Mott proved more than ready to oblige discourse on any subject the game had to offer. Mott and I spent a rainy Southern afternoon talking baseball and rummaging through old photo albums while he provided light-hearted commentary. One particular picture of Mott that captures his spirited nature came from the Elvis Presley film *G.I. Blues*, in which Bitsy enjoyed a "bit part." The photograph showed him sitting on a jeep and slapping his knee in laughter while the King led a group sing-a-long. The happy enthusiasm displayed by Mott in this scene and revealed by the man during our interview, in spite of the fact that he too had been recently hospitalized, was inspiring to say the least. Of course, weakened or not, Bitsy Mott remained on his game, refusing to allow me to leave without first purchasing one of his aluminum can model airplanes, with all proceeds going to his grandson's college fund. This I gladly did. Bitsy is gone now, but I remember him and the others vividly.

It is my hope that this collection of memories will be enjoyed in the vein that it is offered: as a brief look back into the early days of Florida baseball as it was just emerging, and through the eyes of those who lived it. For these men it was the dawn of a new era, the start of a new inning in Florida.

Acknowledgements

The men who share their stories here—Jimmy Bloodworth, Charlie Cuellar, Al Lopez, Bitsy Mott, Manuel Onis, Andy Hansen, Red Barrett and Russ Scarritt—were all gentlemen of the first order. The kindness displayed by each of them and their families, in opening their doors to an eager, fast-talking stranger remains greatly appreciated. They are gone now, but the imprint that they leave behind, one of class, determination and respect, remains. I thank them, will miss them all, and dedicate this effort to them.

Other individuals and groups who have been helpful include Jim Jones at Florida State University; Tony and Bertha Saladino; Ted Webb; Will Benedicks, Monte Finklestein, Mark Goldman, Don Barry and Mary Louise Ellis, all of Tallahassee Community College; Ken Crawford; Bill Kirwin of *Nine*; the Florida Conference of Historians; the Tampa Historical Society; and Gerald Ensley of the *Tallahassee Democrat*. Thanks to each of them.

Adam Watson of the Florida State Archives, Pat Kelly and Ann McFarland of the National Baseball Library and Archives in Cooperstown have all been generous with their time and support in helping to gather images for this volume. Jason Chasteen, commissioning editor for the History Press, and Julie Foster, editorial coordinator, have both supported this project and have gone to great lengths in assisting me during its publication. Victor Doss and Stephen Thompson have helped me with varied technology issues as I prepared the manuscript for print. I appreciate all of their help.

My rather extensive family yields staunch, unflinching support without my asking, and for this I remain grateful: Charles W. Singletary Sr. and Judith A. Corbett; Ray and Judy Fojaco; Manuel and Patricia Zarate; Joe, Amy, Brock, Jake and Alex

Singletary; Lee, Marlene, Tiffany and Taylor Singletary; Lorraine, Frankie and Devin Fernandez; Marjorie Teel; Cliff and Cynthia May; Danny and Marilyn Zarate; Paul and Mary Bachman; Paul Singletary; John David Singletary, a.k.a. the "Nocotee Gator Stomper"; Ray Herrero; Danny Herrero; Lou Herrero; Michelle Highnote; Stan McIntosh; Steve McIntosh; Sam McIntosh; Gloria McIntosh; R.K. and Hazel Singletary; Raymond Singletary; Billy Singletary; Cheri, Calvin, Cy and Casey Jarel; Mark Teel; Rod Teel; and Lauren Teel-Handler. Also the late Bertha L. Singletary, Howard Singletary, Glen McIntosh, Cal and Rose Carter, Raymond Gonzalez and Patrick Michael Foley, who lived for baseball.

My friends and colleagues at the Florida Department of State have also been very encouraging and I thank them: JuDee Pettijohn, Diane Alborn, Sandy Shaughnessy, Susan Stratton, Laura Knight, Allison McCarthy, Suellen Cone, Rivers Buford III, Dave Tepper, Fred Gaske, Jeana Brunson, Courtney Chappell, Marlisha Jackson, Gilda Morris, Gaylen Phillips, Lee Ann Hebenthal, Bea Cotellis, Lori Johnson, Darlene Gordon, Randy Van Oss, Kathy Toon, Karin Stanford, Don Blancett, David Gregory and many others.

Thank you to the following friends across the miles: Todd Thomas, Bob and Robin Lotane, Tyler Turkle, Joel Overton, Stuart Goldberg, Marianne Valenti, Joe and Susan Martelli, De and Chris Rauh, Jimmy and Vicky Bryson, Billy "Boo" Taylor, Pete and Karen Butler, John and Carol Calacino, Rich and Annette Williams, Orlando and Carrie Evora, Mike and Carla Salario, Richard and Lori Crowe, Andy and Lisa Miller, David Clark, Rosemary Giansanti, George and Vicki Drady, Joe and Dawn Bulgarella, Art and Tammy Skafidas, Brian Lynch, Peter Harris, James and Jodee McIver, Lou and Susan Leinhauser, Nick Gray, Jerry and Traci Cash, David Berry, Hillary and Junior Hodges, Robin Barber, Vasili Efimov, Mark Solomon, Fred and Beth Tedio, Fred and Lucy Harris, Ed and Christine Jonas, John Henningsen, Pete Gallagher, Big Scott Harward, the members of the Brookwood School 2003 and 2004 GISA Baseball Georgia State Champions, the late Alex Abaroa, Thierry Kobes and Alone "Ray" Harrison.

Toni Zarate Singletary, my wife of twenty-four years, remains absolutely beautiful. The love and support that she conveys to me on a daily basis is sustaining and it makes me happy; I could not ask for a greater blessing than that. Similarly, our children, Patricia and Nelson—what a feeling it is every day to know that when I get home there they are, with their mother, and living a life that I am a part of. Things are good around our house, I love my family and I am thankful for it.

Al Lopez

> Al Lopez, catcher in the major leagues for 19 years and a manager for 17, was in those days terrific,…always remaining calm, always remaining courtly, always remaining a Tampa guy…the first genuine big-time sports hero from both his native Ybor City and Tampa, and proud of it.
>
> —Tom McEwen, *Tampa Tribune*, October 31, 2005

Alphonso Ramon Lopez, known throughout baseball as El Señor, played Major League baseball for nineteen years. With a lifetime batting average of .261, Lopez proved most valuable to his teams as a catcher. Durability and respect typified his playing days as he established the record for most games caught in a career at 1,918, a record which held for many years. The teams he played for, however, left much to be desired. He was with a first division club a mere nine times, with most of those teams finishing no better than fourth. Contemporaries viewed Lopez as a great low-ball receiver, one of the top handlers of pitchers in the game. He displayed these skills in two All-Star Games, in 1934 and 1941.

Lopez was baseball's first Hispanic manager, and his teams finished first or second in eleven of his first sixteen seasons. Beloved and appreciated by both players and opponents alike, Al Lopez managed by the rule that showing respect gets respect. Lopez often exhibited a superior tactical knowledge of the game, something he attributes to his having played under six Hall of Famers.

His 1954 Cleveland Indians won the American League pennant, going away with a modern Major League record of 111 wins. In 1959 Lopez led an unheralded and seemingly untalented Chicago White Sox squad to his second American League crown. These were the only two teams in sixteen years to overtake the New York Yankees for the American League championship. Upon having completed seventeen seasons as a big-league pilot, El Señor wrapped up his managerial

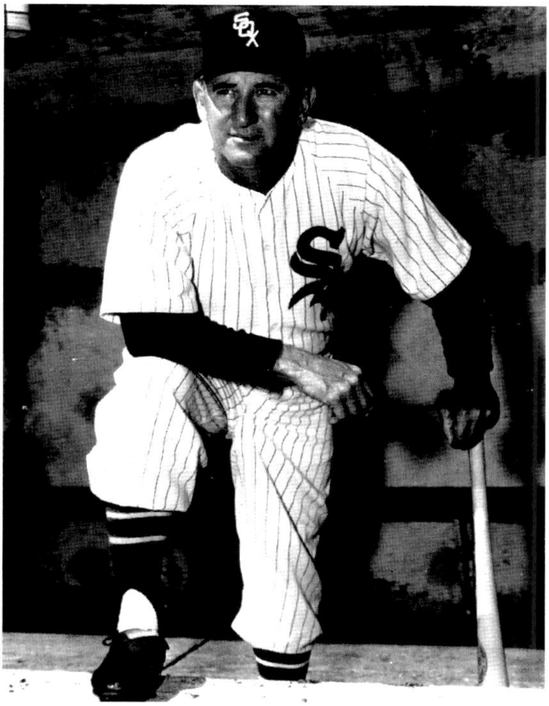

Al Lopez, El Señor. *Courtesy National Baseball Library, Cooperstown, New York.*

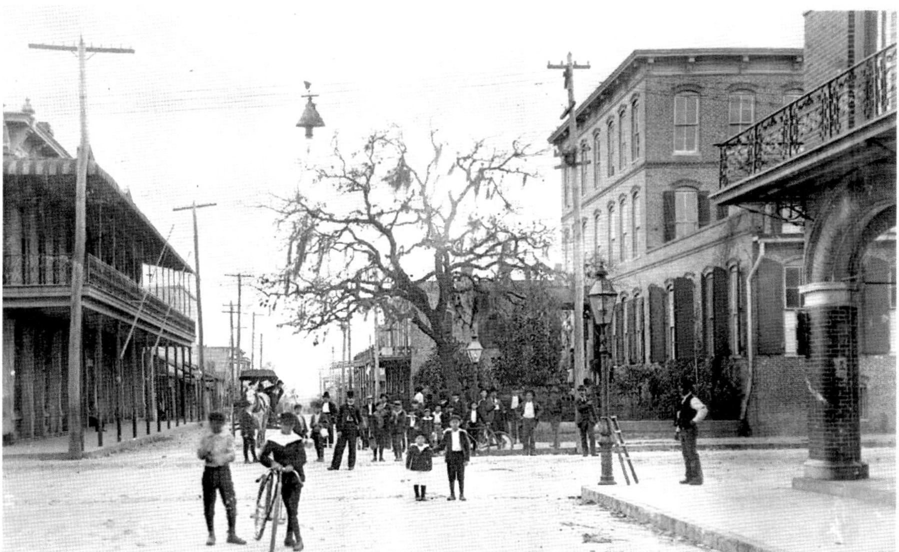

Intersection of Fourteenth Street and Ninth Avenue, Ybor City, Tampa, Florida, ca. 1910. *Courtesy Florida State Archives.*

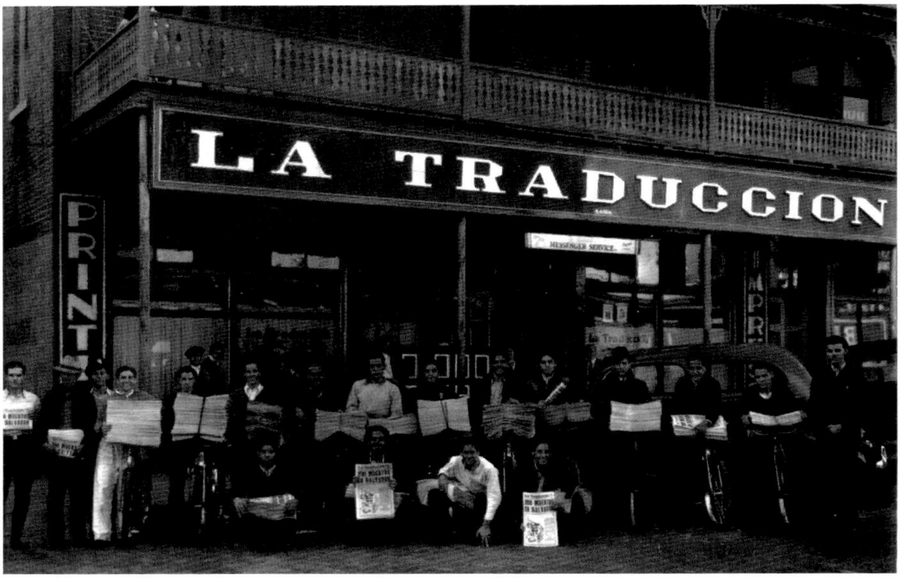

Newsboys for *La Traducción*, the Ybor City Spanish-language newspaper. A reporter from the paper encouraged then-sixteen-year-old Lopez to try out with the Tampa Smokers. *Courtesy Florida State Archives.*

career tied for ninth place on the all-time winning percentage list with a .584 average. In 1977, Al Lopez was enshrined in the Baseball Hall of Fame as a manager.

It was my older brother Emilio, who first got me interested in baseball. He was pretty good too. Emilio had a lot of ability. The difference between he and I was that he wasn't serious enough and he just played for the fun of it. I guess that I was a better competitor; I liked to win. Emilio didn't care one way or the other about winning. He just played to have fun. I started watching him play and I sort of followed him, hoping that I could be as good as or better than he was. He kind of gave me something to shoot at.

I didn't get much coaching or anything like that growing up in Tampa. The Washington Senators used to train here and you had the Tampa Smokers as well. I used to go and watch both of them play, hoping that I could improve by watching them. I did that all through my career—I used to watch people do different things and if it was successful I'd try to do what they did.

There was this sportswriter named Montoto who worked for *La Traduccion*, the Spanish newspaper in Ybor City. One weekend he was covering a series that I was playing in and I

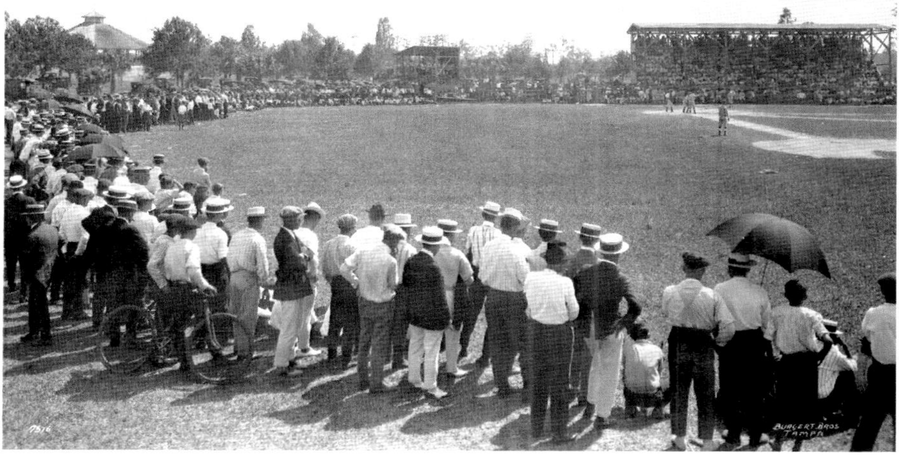

Baseball at McFarlane Park in West Tampa, 1922. *Courtesy Florida State Archives.*

guess that I impressed him. We used to have a Sunday amateur league and I was playing in it at the time. I was only fourteen or fifteen years old and I didn't have any idea that I could play with these older guys. In those days I called guys who were twenty-three and twenty-four "older guys," and they were real good—they played good ball, they never practiced. We just came out on Sunday and played a ballgame. Well, the season ended up in a series between two clubs, my brother was on one of the clubs and I was on the other and we beat them. I happened to have two real good ballgames in the series and after it was over Montoto approached me and asked me if I would go out and practice with the Tampa Smokers, who were just starting to rebuild the ball club. They had folded up the year before due to money and this year they were trying to build it back, 1925.

At that time, the Smokers were a Class D club. They brought in a lot of players who had played in the Class B Virginia League. A lot of under-the-table money was thrown around so they could get the players they needed. Anyway, Montoto sent me with a note down to the Horseshoe pool hall to meet with Doc Nance, who was putting the Smokers back together. When I got there they wouldn't let me in on account of my age so someone went in the back and brought Nance out front. Nance came out front and I

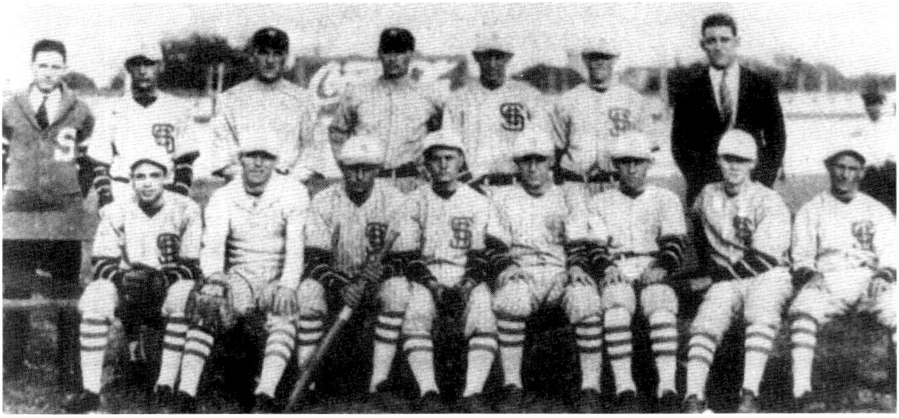

Sacred Heart baseball team Al Lopez (back row, third from right) with Joe Judge and Sam Rice of the Washington Senators on Lopez's right. *Courtesy Al Lopez.*

gave him the note that Montoto had given me and then he asked me how much money I wanted to play for. I told him that I didn't know anything about contracts or any of that and then he asked if $150 a month was OK. I couldn't believe it! I would have played for nothing. Anyway, they signed me to a contract and what benefited me most was that they had to keep two rookies on the club and I was one of the rookies they kept. By the time the playoffs came around, at the end of the season, I was the regular catcher.

The Washington Senators tried to buy my contract from Tampa before the season even started but Tampa wanted too much money. I had caught some batting practice for Washington earlier in the spring and a trainer that they had really took a liking to me. Washington trained in Tampa, and all they usually brought to spring training were those players on the big-league roster including some rookies who they had just bought, three catchers and lots of pitchers. In those days they took batting practice by the hour and three catchers wasn't enough to handle it. So they had asked me if I would just catch batting practice for them and they would give me forty-five dollars a week plus expenses. Well, there again, I would have done it for nothing. Just to put the Washington Senators uniform on was payment enough for me. Also, to be able to learn by catching pitchers like Walter Johnson was great.

You know, I caught Walter Johnson in an exhibition game here in Tampa when I was sixteen years old. Johnson and some other big-league ballplayers were coming through town on a barnstorming tour in 1925. After they got here, they decided that it would be a good idea to have some local ballplayers play with them and they chose me. Well, after

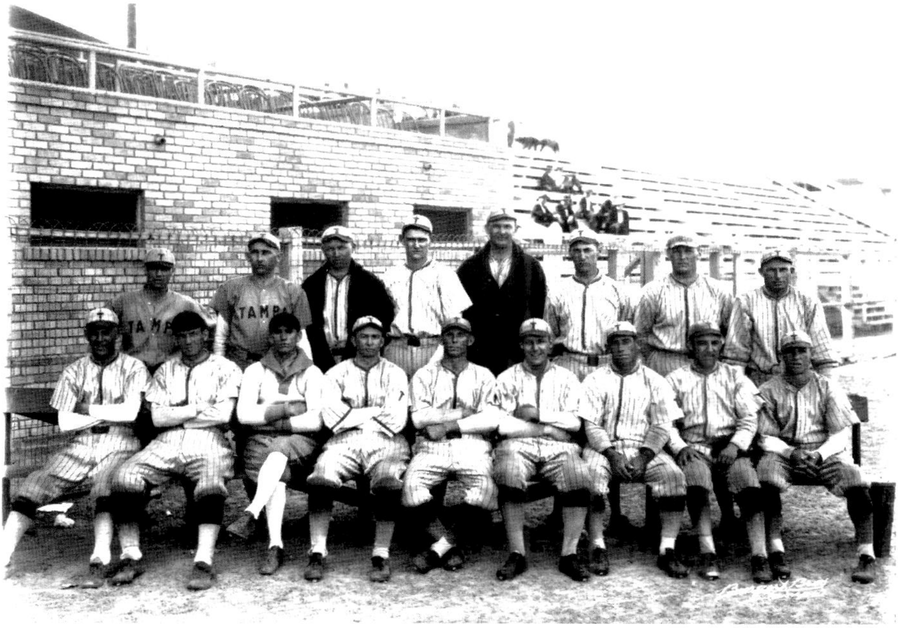

The 1924 Tampa Smokers. *Courtesy Tampa/Hillsborough County Public Library.*

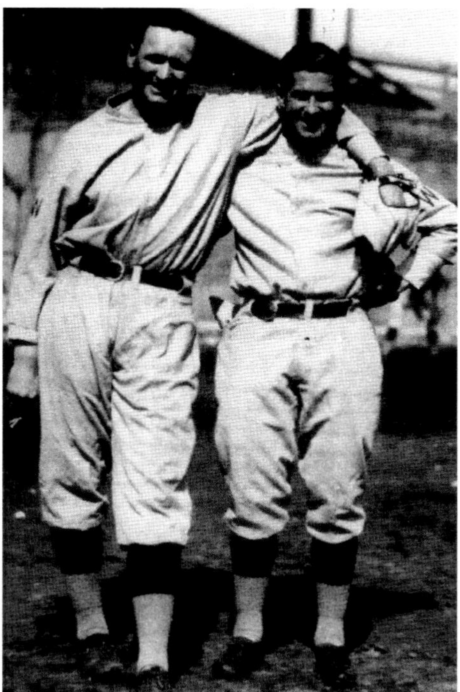

Walter Johnson (left) and Bucky Harris of the Washington Senators, spring training in Tampa, ca. 1920s. *Courtesy Florida State Archives.*

I told them that I'd catch for them, I asked who would be pitching. "Walter Johnson," they said. "Do you think you can catch him?" I said that I didn't know but I would try.

They billed the game as Walter Johnson pitching and Al Lopez catching; can you imagine that? Before the game begins Walter Johnson takes me off to the side and tells me not to call for too many curveballs. I said, "Mr. Johnson, you throw whatever you want to; I'll put down the sign and if you don't want it then shake it off." Johnson told me that the only guys he would let it all out against were Ike Boone and Jack Fournier. These two guys had traditionally given Johnson a tough time at the plate. Well the game started and I caught him good. After the game was over, Johnson told some people that I did real well back there; handled myself fine.

There weren't many Hispanic ballplayers or ballplayers from Florida playing professional ball when I came up. My first year with Tampa, 1925, they had two besides myself. One Cuban boy, Oscar Estrada, they brought him in; he played the outfield, pitched and played first base. Good player. He was sold to the Boston Braves after the season. The other fellow I luckily roomed with, named Cesare Alvarez. He was an old man, about thirty-two. He had been pitching quite a while. Alvarez spoke English, but, you know, English like I did I guess, broken. Cesare had married a Spanish girl from Tampa and she had her family here. While on the road, we would go out at night to eat or to a movie, because we played all day games, then get up in the morning, have breakfast, go over to the ballpark and play our game.

When I played in the minor leagues I never minded the travel. When you're young and all, you think that's fun. The minor leagues after that got pretty tough traveling

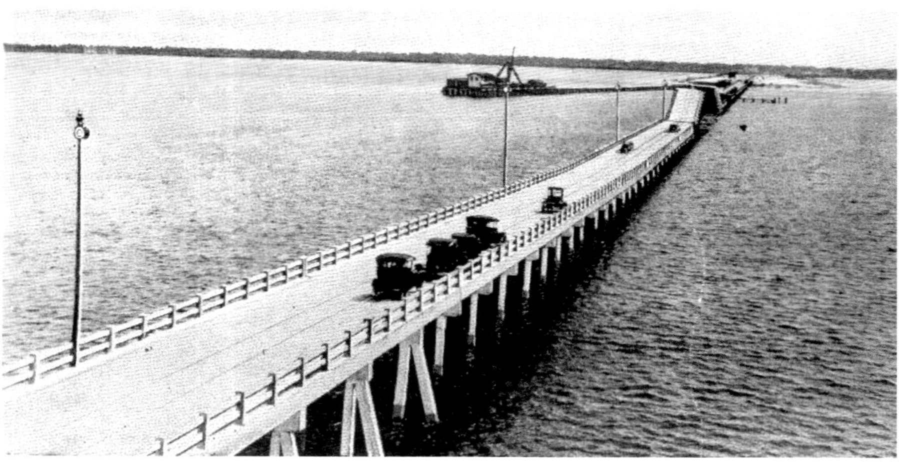

Gandy Bridge, spanning Tampa Bay from Pinellas County. *Courtesy Florida State Archives.*

because they travel in buses. I was very fortunate because I think Sanford was the longest jump. We had Sarasota, Lakeland, St. Petersburg and Bradenton in our league. We did all the travel by private car.

St. Petersburg was the easiest route because of Gandy Bridge. But before the bridge was built, we used to take Memorial Highway and go up around Clearwater, Largo, in there, just to get to St. Pete. It was about sixty miles and a terrible drive. Memorial Highway was just one-lane pavement. If another car was coming from the other direction, you would have to slow down and give him half of the road. Lakeland was another terrible trip. Tampa to Lakeland was a tough drive in those days. You had to pass through Mango, Seffner, Kissimmee and then into Orlando, the other side of Lakeland, just to get there.

We usually had pretty good crowds in those parks once we got there. We'd have 1,000 to 1,500 people at the games, but the prices were cheap. They were collecting $1,000 a game, maybe a little more than that. At the end of the year a team might get lucky and break even. If they broke even during the season then they would profit if they sold one player.

When I went to Jacksonville we traveled by train most of the time. Then I went to the South Atlantic League with Macon and that was train. Atlanta traveled by train and that was great compared to like they do now. We used to play all day games in those days, there were no lights, and we played all day games at three o'clock. Now they might play a twilight double-header, jump back on the bus and travel four hundred miles for tomorrow's game. So we actually had it easier back then. I was very lucky.

There were very few Hispanics playing professional baseball in this country at that time. Cuba was the one that was producing the ballplayers. The Dominican Republic has recently done a remarkable job, because now there are a lot of Major League ballplayers from there. But back then, the Dominican Republic might have had a few. Mexico had one or two. Aparicio and Carascal came later from Venezuela. Luis Aparicio's uncle, I think, used to pitch in the big leagues.

Back in 1928, 1929, 1930 is when they started bringing in the players from Cuba. There was a scout on the Washington club that used to go down there and scout young ballplayers and bring them to Washington. The first clubs to bring in Latin ballplayers at all were the New York Giants and Cincinnati Reds. Adolfo Luque is a good example. He was from Cuba, the "Pride of Havana" they called him. He came up with Cincinnati but played a lot of years with the Giants and then some with Brooklyn. Luque was a smart pitcher. He was still with the Dodgers when I came up with them and I learned a lot from him.

Cincinnati had another guy, Rafael Almeida I think it was, a third baseman that came from a wealthy family. He didn't like the traveling so one day he just got off the train and went back home to Cuba. I guess he got homesick or something. They said he was a very fine ballplayer. Luque was a fine pitcher. Mike Gonzalez, a catcher, was another good one.

You know, I think the news media made more of Jackie Robinson's problems than there actually was. Yes, there was some riding, they rode me, not just the black players, and they rode the American players and if you can't stand the heat, then get out. There was plenty of riding in those days. I think that the news media was the one who really created this thing. Jackie Robinson weighed about 220 pounds; he was a hell of an athlete. Fight? I imagine he could fight, he was strong, he could run, do everything, he was a great athlete. You mean to say that somebody had to feel sorry because somebody was going to pick on him? If it was me, named Lopez, weighing 160 pounds, I could see it. He was mature enough to handle it. He was already twenty-four or twenty-five before he got to the Majors.

I don't know anything about any death threats or poor living conditions. I do know that Larry Doby was a great player who let it affect him. If Doby hadn't had that feeling where he thought everybody was against him or that he was fighting everybody, Doby could have been a Hall of Famer. I think Larry was under a lot of pressure but some of it he placed there himself. Doby became a great outfielder and had tremendous power and he was a good hitter—could do everything—but that constant pressure on him really hurt his chance to become the ballplayer he should have been. He was good; there was nothing wrong with Larry Doby, good ballplayer. [Larry Doby was subsequently elected to the Baseball Hall of Fame.]

Anyway, getting back to the Smokers, we had another local guy named Mike Boza who could really hit but he never made it past that level. It's hard trying to determine who will make it and who won't. You know a lot of people will look at a young ballplayer and say that kid should be in the Majors. But for some reason or other, I don't know if it's the heart or brain or what, a lot of them don't develop the way they should. Ability wise, there are a lot of kids that you see and think that kid's really got talent. It happens, you pay some guy $100,000 to sign and they never make it. Mike Boza was a good hitter. All he cared about was hitting, but in those days you don't just hit, you have to be able to play a position and that is what hurt him.

Our purpose in those days was to win the ballgame. A lot of people think all that you look for is a hitter. But you had to win the ballgame first, and hitting was a big part of it but not everything. I think the media has made batting averages and home runs seem so important that hitting is all many ballplayers think about. Nowadays they even get paid based on it. To me, as a manager, I didn't look just at the guy who was hitting .300. If he was hitting .300 but didn't help you any other way, I couldn't use him. I would rather have a guy who could field and help me all the way around. Defense is the big thing.

There is a question that I'm asked all the time. Who was the greatest pitcher I ever caught? Dazzy Vance was a great pitcher with Brooklyn. As I told you, I caught Walter Johnson in a practice game here. Bob Feller was another great pitcher. I managed him late in his career. Dizzy Dean, I caught in the 1934 All-Star Game in New York. It's a pretty hard choice. You look at guys like Lefty Grove. I hit against him in spring games. To me he was easy to hit against. In the spring I guess he wasn't really, you know, giving it his best. But I talked to Charlie Gehringer who was with Detroit, super ballplayer. He hit against Johnson, maybe when Johnson was already starting to go down, and against Grove and he thought Grove was just as fast as Johnson was. That surprised me.

Zach Wheat really impressed me as a hitter. He was also a fine gentleman. The year I was catching batting practice for Washington, 1925, I went to Clearwater with the team and sat in the dugout watching the ballplayers. I didn't know Zach Wheat, never heard of him. But when I saw him at the plate I just couldn't believe it. He was a picture at the plate hitting. You could see his jaws were tight. Wheat stood in there and not only dug into the batter's box with his back foot but with his front foot as well. The only guy I ever saw do that. He was a good hitter. They loved him in Brooklyn.

Brooklyn is the Major League club that eventually signed me out of the minor leagues. After having played in Tampa for two seasons I was drafted by Jacksonville, a Class B club. You could only play two years in one league before becoming subject to the draft. So the Jacksonville team, which had just started the year before, drafted me to come up. I had a pretty good year at Jacksonville, hit .276 with some triples and homers in there.

Jacksonville is where the scouts first started to take notice of me. We had a pitcher by the name of Ben Cantwell. Cantwell was having a great year, a record of 25–5 or close to it by the early part of July. He would have won 40 games had he pitched there all season long. All the big-league scouts at that time would come out to see him. In those days each team had only a few scouts and they would send those scouts into wherever a ballplayer was hot. Every time we played we must have had six to eight scouts in the stands watching, especially when Cantwell was pitching. For some reason or another, the Brooklyn scout, fellow by the name of Nap Rucker, took a liking to me. He notified the front office about me and said that he liked the catcher better than the pitcher. They told him if he liked the catcher to go ahead and buy him. So they made a deal for me for $10,000 and I was sold to the Brooklyn Dodgers.

At the time they only gave the Jacksonville guy $1,000 down and said that the rest would follow if they kept me. The Jacksonville guy told me that he would let me have a tenth of it if I made good. I said that's fine. I never did get anything.

The next season at Macon was kind of my breakthrough year you could say. I batted over .300 and caught over a hundred games. At the end of the season Brooklyn called

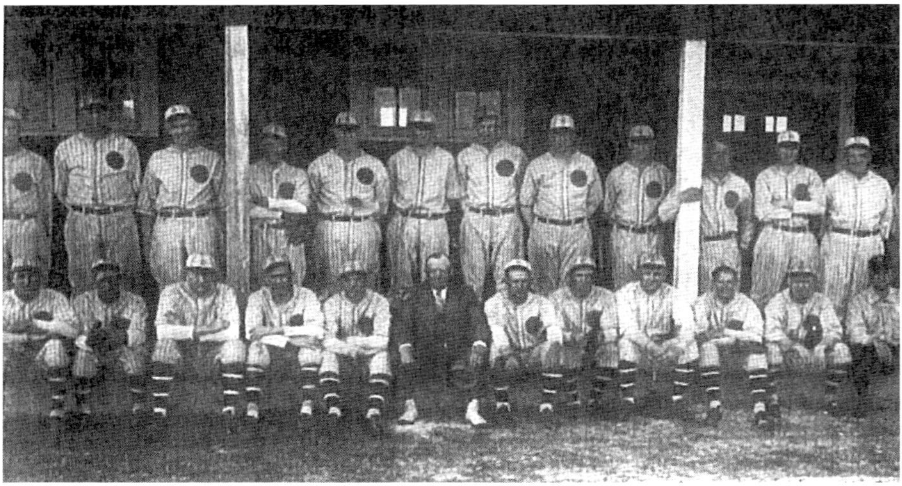

The Brooklyn 'Robins," with Wilbert Robinson front row center, Clearwater, Florida, 1927. Dazzy Vance is sitting front row, third from left, while Burleigh Grimes stands in rear, fourth from right. *Courtesy Florida State Archives.*

me up to the Majors. Coming from Tampa and having played only in small towns like Jacksonville and Macon, I was amazed when I got to Brooklyn. I got off at the station and luckily I ran into two guys that belonged to Brooklyn and had just been called up from Atlanta. It was lucky for me because I was only eighteen years old and had never been anywhere like New York. We took the subway, one of the players had been there before, and we rode underneath the river, and up at the Brooklyn side we got off. It was the first station we came to and by God there was a hotel right on top of the station, quite an experience.

Well, it was pretty much the end of the season when I got there and I sat around on the bench, not doing anything much until the last weekend series of the year. We were playing the Pirates and all of a sudden Wilbert Robinson, the manager, put me in to catch. I found out later that the reason I caught was because Burleigh Grimes, the last of the great spitball pitchers, was facing us that day and none of the other catchers liked to face him. Burleigh Grimes was kind of mean when he took the mound.

Anyway, I caught that day and went 0 for 4. The next day we had a double-header and "Robbie" let me catch both ends. This is when the Pirates had Pie Traynor and Glen Wright on the left side of their infield. Well, I was strictly a pull hitter and I hit some good hard shots to the left side. I'd take off for first, figuring I had myself a hit, but each time, to my astonishment, I saw that peg zinging into the first baseman's glove. I knew, I just

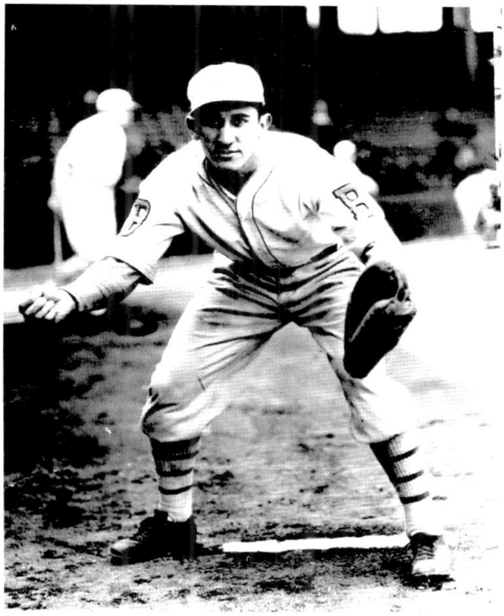

A youthful Al Lopez with the Brooklyn Dodgers, ca. 1930. *Courtesy National Baseball Library, Cooperstown, New York.*

knew, that at Macon those would have been hits. It was practically impossible to hit a ball past Traynor and Wright. I was 0 for 8 in that double-header and went home that fall wondering what a fellow had to do to get a base hit in the big leagues.

The next season I was promoted to the Atlanta Crackers in the Southern Association. I had another good season there, batting over .300, hit with some power and did most of the catching. It was in Atlanta that I began to realize that I wasn't making as much money as some of the other guys. I think this was on account of my age and inexperience. When I was in Atlanta there were some guys making as much as $1,000 a month while I was making $575 a month. The clubs made a little bit of money but then the Depression hit and a lot of those minor league clubs went under. A man named Colonel Spiller owned the Atlanta club. He owned both the club and the ballpark. Anyway, when the Depression hit, your bargaining power went out the door because their argument was, "We don't know how long we can last." It was true; a lot of clubs went under. After that season I was called up to Brooklyn again.

You know, Wilbert Robinson was an old catcher himself. He'd caught for the Baltimore Orioles and he came up as a coach for John McGraw. McGraw had been a teammate of his at Baltimore and of course McGraw became a legend in New York. As manager of the Giants, McGraw had the privilege of doing everything. He ran the whole outfit for years and was greatly admired, even by the opposing players. I think he was the first manager to start playing the modern-day baseball, you know, hitting behind the runner and ideas like that. Wilbert Robinson coached under McGraw and then he became the manager at Brooklyn and then I went there.

Robinson had some success with Brooklyn. He managed the Dodgers in 1920 when they played in the World Series against Cleveland. Tris Speaker was the manager for Cleveland and Robinson managed the Dodgers. He was a nice man. Robbie was almost like a father to me. He treated me nice and he always wanted me to sit next to him my first full year with the team, 1930. Just sit there so we could talk things over. He'd watch the ballgame and I'd sit next to him. In those days Robbie would bring in tin packs of Lucky Strike tobacco—they used to give it to him—and he would sit it next to him. He would wear pinstriped pants and a silk shirt with a tie to manage. He also wore two-tone shoes. He'd hang his sport coat up in the dugout. In those days you'd pay forty or fifty dollars for a sport coat, and that was a lot of money because you could buy a suit for eighteen. Robbie used to wear expensive clothes.

Robbie was a big guy and he had a scar on his face. He also had false teeth, upper and lower. He used to come in there and before the game he'd open up and start chewing tobacco. As the inning progressed he put more and more tobacco in his mouth. If it was a long inning, you can imagine he'd have a mouth full of tobacco. So, he would spit it all out and go to the fountain—we used to have a little fountain with a spigot for water—he'd go over there and take both of his plates out and wash them off there all over the fountain. We wouldn't drink water off that spigot for the rest of the day.

But again, he was a nice man. I thought he was great with pitchers too. Wilbert Robinson and Bill McKechnie were the best managers for pitchers that I played under. We had some good ballplayers on that club, that is for sure: Dazzy Vance, Watty Clark, Del Bissonette and Glen Wright, who was a great shortstop that had come over from Pittsburgh. Jake Flowers played second base; Wally Gilbert was at third, Rube Bressler in left field, Johnny Frederick in center and Babe Herman in right.

We had a good ball club! It was up and down all year between the Cubs, Giants, Cardinals and our club. All these clubs were up and down all season long until finally the Cardinals put on a late streak and won the pennant. I think they beat the A's that year in the World Series. They beat a great club, the Philadelphia Athletics.

That first season I realized that I was a young rookie coming up, and I just tried to catch the same way I had been. They must have liked my style of play because they signed me. I used to backup first base on throws, a lot of hustle—I was small—and I'd always run to first base to backup the play. One day an umpire asked me, "What are you doing running in back of first base like that, you're holding up the game, they don't overthrow like that!" He was wrong. They overthrow all right. That umpire wanted to keep the game going faster.

The Brooklyn club, my first year or two, was my favorite because it had a bunch of guys that were great players. In 1930, Del Bissonette hit .330; Jake Flowers, .320; Glen Wright, a shortstop hitting fourth in the order, batted .321; Johnny Frederick, .334; Babe Herman hit .393 and didn't even win the batting title. We had a good hitting ball club.

Let me see, who won the batting title that year? Babe Herman had the year before, no, I think in 1929 Babe Herman hit .381 and Lefty O'Doul beat him out by batting .398. The next year, 1930, Babe Herman hit .390 or something, I think .393, and Bill Terry hit .401 to beat him. Can you imagine putting up two years in a row like that and not winning a batting title?

After all of that offense, the league got together and changed the ball. I think it was 1931 when they changed it. They wanted to deaden the ball. It was a mistake to do it. John McGraw is the one who complained about the lively ball and moved to deaden it. He couldn't play his brand of baseball with that lively ball. You know, inside baseball. Everyone was hitting home runs and stuff like that. But I think going to a dead ball hurt the game. The year after they changed the ball, Bill Terry, who had hit .401 in 1930, dropped down to .340. There were three guys bunched together—Chick Hafey, Chuck Klein and Bill Terry—and Hafey won it by percentage points. I had batted .309 in 1930 and dropped to .269 the next season, so they cut my salary. I think that is a big reason why they did it. They wanted to cut down on player salaries.

You know, when I played with the Boston Braves in 1937, we had the most amazing thing happen. The club finished in fifth place, but they had two twenty-game winners. Jim Turner and Lou Fette, two rookies who had both been around a little while, both turned in twenty-win seasons. They both came up when they were over thirty years of age. I enjoyed catching them because they were both ground-ball pitchers and had good control. It made for quick ballgames.

The toughest pitcher to catch that I ever played with was Van Lingle Mungo. Mungo wasn't just fast, but he was wild. You'd give him a target high and he'd throw it low and away. He hit me on the instep one day after I'd given him a high target. I wanted to pitch the batter high inside with two strikes and Mungo hit me right on the instep, with a man on third base! Luckily the ball hit on the instep, because I was able to save the run. I looked out there at him and he was laughing like hell because he hit me.

Once, in 1938, while I was playing in Boston, a hurricane came blowing into town right in the middle of a ballgame. That wind picked up so much that a pop fly was hit to shallow left-center and Tony Cuccinello, at shortstop, thought he was going to get it, but by God I ended up making the catch by the dugout and I caught it foul. The umpire ended up calling the game on account of "inclement weather." The wind was blowing I guess forty-five or fifty miles an hour while we were out there playing. We had tried to get the umpire to call it earlier. You know how hurricane weather is, cloudy and the wind blowing. We knew it was coming. The umpire says, "No, it was announced to play a double-header and we got to make an attempt to play a second game, that's a league rule. But if it gets any worse I call the game." By the time they called the game and we were able to get downtown the wind was blowing over a hundred miles an hour. Commonwealth Avenue in Boston is beautiful, with sidewalks and a walk-thing in the middle. It had one-way lanes going in both directions and these big elm trees were on both sides of the street. That storm topped those trees just like matchsticks.

I suffered a bad thumb injury that same season in Boston. It was like when you take a chicken bone and pop it at the joint, the same thing. My thumb was hit by a foul tip and right away it goes numb. It didn't hurt though, no pain on it. I put my hand behind my back and took my mask off and was reaching to take my protector off when here comes Stengel. Casey Stengel was managing Boston by then. "What's wrong Al?" I said, "I think I got a busted thumb, Casey." Casey says, "Let me see it." I say, "I don't want to look at it, Casey." He says, "Let me see it." So, I had to show it to him and he puked right there on the spot.

It was bad. They wanted to carry me off the field but I said I can walk. I didn't want to look at it, so finally we walked into the dugout and they called a doctor from the stands and he told them to take me in the clubhouse. "Carry him in the clubhouse," he says. I say, "I can walk." So I walked in the clubhouse and went in the trainer's room and still I hadn't looked at it. I turned my head away while the doctor took all the gauze he could and wrapped it—my whole hand had to be wrapped to keep the dust off it. Anyway, the doctor told them to call for the club doctor, O'Brien, and O'Brien says for them to bring me to the hospital real quick.

So they brought me to the hospital. I went in uniform. Two guys drove me. They wanted me to take an ambulance but I told them to forget it and just get me over there. I figured they would put a couple of stitches in it and I would be back in no time. Well, we got there and as soon as Dr. O'Brien cut the gauze off he says, "Get the operating room ready." My God, I stayed in the hospital three days. I was on the disabled list about six weeks. But then as soon as it was over I went back to catching.

I was lucky to get back that quick. I'll tell you what he did. When my thumb was still tender, O'Brien took it and bent it over as far as he could so it would grow like a claw. That way, if it healed stiff I would still be able to throw the ball. He was thinking about my livelihood. He used a metal splint, not wooden, that bent over. I thought it was a real good idea. I used to have a little better play in it than I got now.

When I played for Boston, the Braves were a good club. We didn't have any powerful hitters, but that was by design I think. It was a big ballpark so you went inside for your runs. I think Braves Field was the worst ballpark to hit in that there was. No question about it. No question! The wind blew in, the background was bad and the infield was

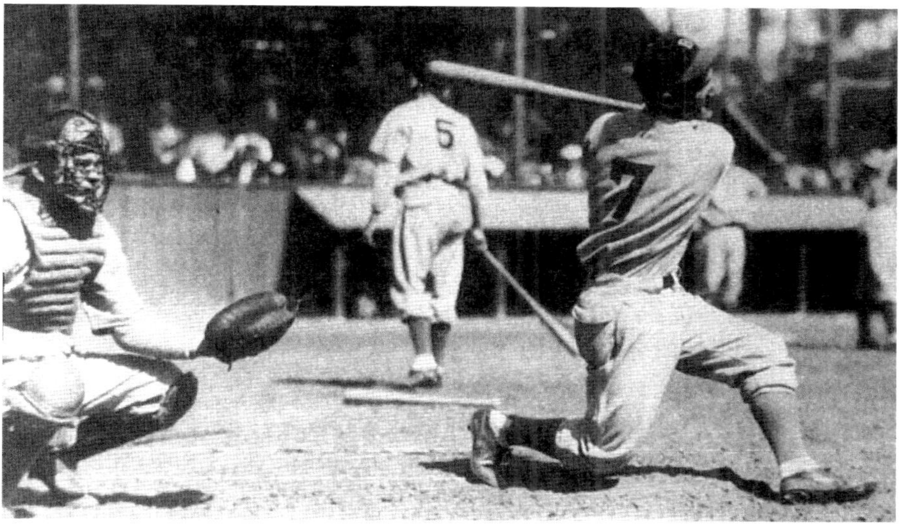

Lopez batting for the Boston Braves. *Courtesy Al Lopez.*

soaked all the time. Everything was against the hitter. It was a good place to catch because you could play a ballgame in an hour and twenty minutes. You'd be out of there. We'd have 2–1, 3–1 ballgames. That was how Fette and Turner won twenty games in 1937. We had another guy on the club, Danny McFayden, that won 14 games the same season and he pitched as good as those guys. Yeah, Danny McFayden could pitch, by God.

Our manager, Bill McKechnie, was named manager of the year that season, 1937. Then he left and went to Cincinnati. That burned up the owner. He got mad as could be because McKechnie was well thought of in Boston. That is when he comes up with Casey Stengel. That was the second time I had Stengel. I had played for him in Brooklyn and now Boston.

You know, Casey traded me both times. The other time I was traded, not by Casey but when I left Pittsburgh, I had asked them to trade me because Billy Herman was coming in there as manager. I asked Pittsburgh to trade me for a reason. The newspapers had a fan poll asking the fans to pick the next manager of the Pirates and I won the poll by majority. So, I told the Pittsburgh brass that the best thing to do was to get me off the club so as to give Herman a chance. This was Pittsburgh, 1946. That winter they had made the trade to get Billy Herman from Boston, they gave up Jumbo Elliott, Jim Russell and they got Herman and somebody else in the deal.

When Casey traded me away from Boston, they announced that they got $40,000 and Ray Berres. The team needed cash real bad because they just didn't have any money. Personally, I think they got more than that. A lot more, but they only announced that. Ray Berres was on the other end of both of those trades. Later on he became my pitching coach at Chicago and we are very close friends. Very close friends. But Stengel was the one who traded me off both times.

There is no question that the pounding I took catching and my durability behind the plate affected my hitting. You know, catchers maybe might hit another ten or fifteen points higher if they were playing other positions. I don't know if I would have or not; I'm not looking for alibis. I think that you just get run down, you're catching double-headers in St. Louis and Cincinnati and its 110 or 112 degrees and you're playing day games, no night games in those days. After a while, ten years in or so, I started catching one game on double-headers and they'd put somebody else in there.

There are some kids coming up today that are real good catchers. They have good arms—although they have to, the way they are running today. I think they run more in baseball now than ever. My only problem with today's catchers is the way so many of them catch on their knees. Also, I think the way they position their hands is a problem. There are more passed balls now than I've ever seen. I went one entire year with no passed balls and another year with only one. Now, these catchers, most of them, have ten, twelve, fifteen passed balls, and there is no reason for it.

I think they're just holding their hands in a bad position. They're catching one-handed; they put their glove hand out front. I used to catch by bringing everything back into my body. I always used two hands doing it. Now of course you get hit in the fingers a lot more, but you keep the pitch in front of you. Also, when they catch the ball with one hand out in front, then they have to bring the ball all the way back to throw. We used to catch it and throw it all in one motion.

The mitts were a lot different then too. They had padding all around a small pocket. They were made for two-handed catching. Now they're coming up with a little bitty glove. I have seen some catchers use gloves that look like a first-base mitt. And what about the lazy footwork of these guys? Have you seen the catchers on the side of their feet? Some of them are even sitting down on the ground to give a target. How are you going to get up to field a swinging bunt if you're sitting down behind the plate? I used to be out there to take the bunts myself. The pitchers on my team didn't have to worry about fielding bunts because that was my job.

There were three great catchers when I was in the league. Oh yeah, there were good catchers then. Gabby Hartnett was great with the Cubs—great arm, one of the best arms I ever saw. Mickey Cochrane with Philadelphia and Bill Dickey with New York, both are Hall of Famers and they were both catching then. Bill Dickey had a good arm. I think the weakest arm of the three was Mickey Cochrane. If Mickey Cochrane would have had a better arm there is no telling how great he would have been. He had a good bat though. They like to compare Johnny Bench to this group of guys and Johnny Bench was great. I didn't see Bench play that much but my God, he could throw—good receiver, good hands. I'm surprised that he said that his legs bothered him that much because all those others guys, Hartnett and Cochrane and myself, we all caught a lot.

As good as Bench was, he didn't stay around long enough to pass my record for most games caught. There are a lot of people who thought he would. He played over two thousand games, but many were at third or first. Bob Boone always had a chance at the record because he caught very little in the minors, I think one year. He was a third baseman at school—what the hell school did he go to, Stanford I think. The Phillies signed him and made him a catcher and he was a good catcher. Boone was a good catcher. He could receive real good. Jim Hegan, my old catcher at Cleveland was a great receiver. He and Boone were a lot alike. Of the young guys Boone could handle the ball easier than the rest.

You can see, most of these guys, what they do is they drop their glove hand out in front and then reach up and snatch it. Any time you see a guy kind of flipping with his hands, he is not a good receiver. For you to be a good receiver, same with an infielder, you got to have smoothness. Sometimes you will see an infielder go to field a ground ball and it takes a bad hop and he snatches at it. You can't do that. You have got to have smoothness. It is the same way with catching. Hell, if you are a good receiver there is nothing to it.

In 1940 I was traded to Pittsburgh, and you can say it kind of gave me a new life. I liked to play in Pittsburgh; the ballpark was nice to play in. Good ballpark to hit in. It was a lot better playing there than in Braves Field in Boston. We had a pretty good ball club. I think we finished third that year, I'm not sure. Arky Vaughan and I went to the All-Star Game in 1941. That was the game where Ted Williams hit the home run off the face of the roof to win it for the American League.

Tony Cuccinello was a teammate of mine in Brooklyn and Boston and my longtime assistant with Cleveland and Chicago. He is also a very good friend of mine. Tony was always a good ballplayer. He was a pretty good hitter, fine on double plays, but lacked a great arm or great speed. If he had better speed he would have been maybe a Hall of Famer. He just couldn't run very well. He was a good player to have on a team. You could win a pennant with him playing.

Tony and I were roommates and after that we became closer, good friends. When I got my first managing job at Indianapolis, the first thing I asked the owner for was that he allow me to hire Tony as a coach. I needed a coach because I was going to have to catch some ballgames myself—I caught about fifty games at Indianapolis—and I'd need someone to do the coaching while I was in there. Tony came over and he was a great help to me my first year managing at Indianapolis.

Then the Cincinnati club comes over and asks me if they can have permission to talk with him about going back to the big leagues. I told them that if Tony can go back

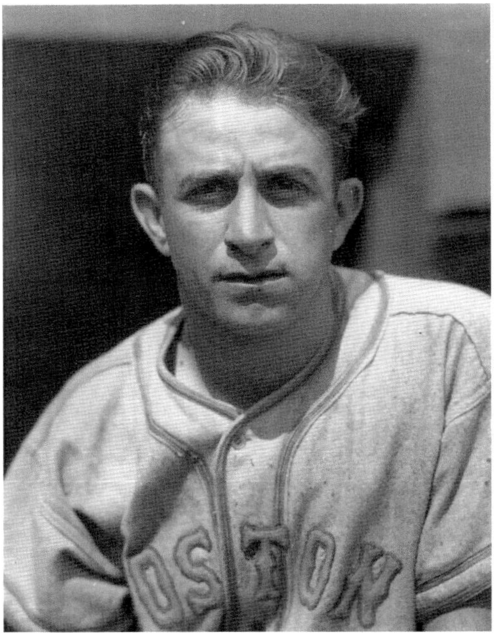

Tony Cuccinello "You could win a pennant with him playing." *Courtesy National Baseball Library, Cooperstown, New York.*

to the big leagues, I won't stand in his way. So he went to Cincinnati. Later, when I got the Cleveland job, Tony wanted to come over with me, so I tried to get him back but Cincinnati still wanted him. Tony said, "Next year, regardless." He had already signed his contract. He told me, "Regardless, Al, next year I'm coming with you." So he finally did. In 1952 he came and joined me at Cleveland and he was a big help.

I played with a lot of good ballplayers over the years. I've already mentioned Van Lingle Mungo. He was something else. If he got mad, he was mad. You know, he was one of those guys who got into trouble a lot on account of his drinking, a real outspoken guy. But, he was a good friend of mine. To me he was a real nice guy. You know, he respected me and that was great. We got along real good. And Mungo always had a lot of talent; there was no doubt about that.

Ernie Lombardi was with us for a while in Brooklyn before they traded him to Cincinnati. He was green at the time. Ernie had just come up to the big leagues. He was green and he was sitting on the bench. I think he might have been a lot better than what he showed at Brooklyn if he would have had a chance to catch. But he was catching only once in a while and that's a tough job. As soon as they traded him over to Cincinnati he became a great catcher. Brooklyn couldn't try him at another position because he was so slow. He couldn't run at all. Ernie was slow and catcher

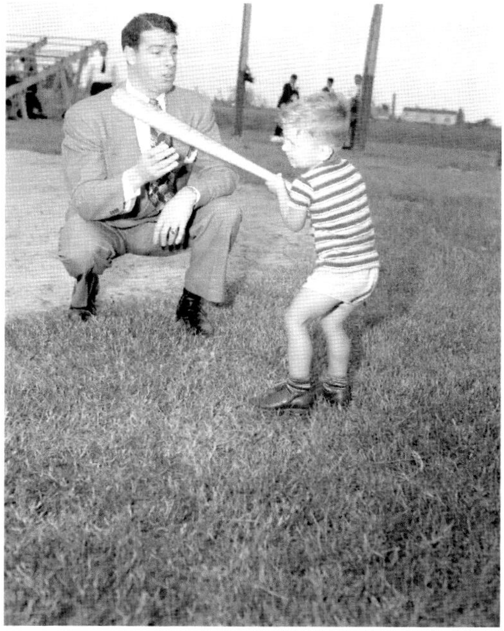

Joe DiMaggio poses with a young slugger, 1948. *Courtesy Florida State Archives.*

was the only position he could have played. He became a great catcher and a hell of a good hitter. He led the league in hitting twice, I think.

Vince DiMaggio was my roommate in Pittsburgh. The difference between Vince and his brother Joe was hitting. But I mean his brother was *Joe DiMaggio*. Who was going to keep up with a kid brother like that? Vince was all right, though. He would have been a good ballplayer in this era because he struck out a lot. I think he struck out 110 times one season. But he could hit home runs. He hit twenty-something home runs and he was a great fielder, he just struck out too much. But today, he would have been an outstanding ballplayer. He could have played for Sparky Anderson on the Tigers. In those days they'd say jeez, he strikes out 110 or 115 times. Today they strike out 140 to 150 times and don't even play the field if they are the designated hitter. The guy that Detroit had, Rob Deer, he struck out about 180 times. Vince would have been right at home in today's game.

I caught Rip Sewell's two best years, 1943 and 1944. He was on the staff the whole seven years I was there at Pittsburgh. He threw that ephus pitch, the blooper. It was something he used to fool around with and the media and the fans liked it. He had a theory that you had to put a certain spin on the ball so that the ball would go up there and come straight down, you know. It was just kind of a bloop ball; it went as high as that ceiling. It was a legitimate pitch. The first time he threw it, he threw it for a strike on Dom Dellasandro, a real small guy. Dom was only about five-six and Rip threw a strike, or at least the umpire thought so.

He called Dom out. Dellasandro says, "You're a damn liar, that ball was way up there." I thought it was a strike. I caught it right on the ground as usual.

Al Rosen is a great, great fellow and a nice guy to have on a team. He was a real good team man; still a friend of mine. He did a great job as general manager for San Francisco and he did a great job for us in Cleveland. Al Rosen came real close to winning the Triple Crown in 1953. He led the league in RBIs, led the league in home runs and just missed getting the batting title. Al lost the batting title on a controversial call during the final game of the season. The umpire said that he missed first base on an infield grounder and that allowed Mickey Vernon to beat him out by percentage points. The umpire later said that if Al had hit the bag he would have called him safe. He had a chance to be a Triple Crown guy. Al was a good guy, a real fine man to have on the team.

Early Wynn was a great competitor. He won twenty-some-odd games every year. How could you dislike him? But he was a competitor. I had a rule in the clubhouse that even if you pitch like a dog I am going to go out there in a nice way and ask you for the ball, pat you on the back and you can go in. If you have something to argue about, wait until we get to the clubhouse. When I go out there, I'm not going to show you up so don't show me up. Well, this one day he was arguing with the umpire and when I asked for the ball he threw it and hit me right in the stomach. Threw it sounds too strong, he just kind of flipped it at me. I said, "Give me the damn ball and don't be throwing it at me!" After the game he came into my office and apologized. I said, "Early, I know how you feel, but the people upstairs, the news media and the fans don't know that. They think you're mad at me, you mad at me?" He says, " Oh no." I used to tell them don't get mad at me because I come out there to take you out; I hate to take you out. Let me sit in the dugout and mind my own business. Get those guys out. It's nice to sit in the dugout. I'd tell them to get mad at those guys who are hitting.

They tell a story about Early Wynn, that he was arguing with the umpire you know, and he was having a bad day and I had already gone out to talk with him. In baseball if you go out twice in the same inning then the pitcher is automatically out the second time. So he kept getting into trouble and finally I went out there to lift him. After he saw me coming he started going at the umpire again and the umpire told him, "One more word out of you and you are going to be gone. I hate to throw you out but you'll be gone." Early says to the umpire, "What do you think Lopez is coming out here for, to bring me a ham sandwich?"

Bob Lemon was a great pitcher, another good guy to have on a club. Hell of a pitcher and a good hitter too. I always felt that he was going to last quite a while because he had initially come up as a third baseman and an outfielder. The wear on his arm was not that great. Lemon started pitching in the middle of 1946. He saved Bob Feller's no-hitter one time with a great catch in the outfield. He didn't last that long though. He came up with chips in his elbow. It was the way he threw the ball. He had a terrific sinker. The way he

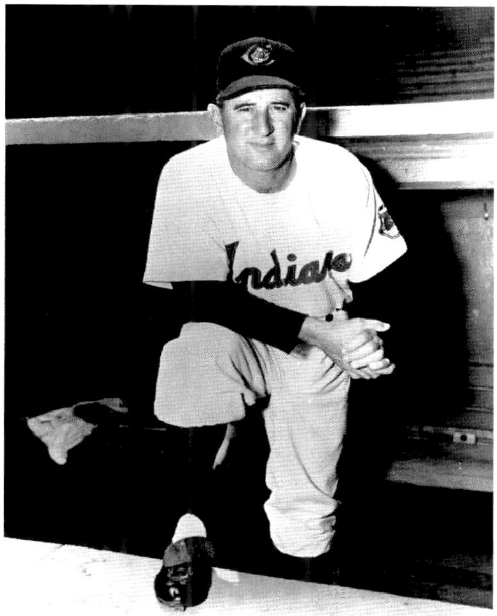

Al Lopez, "the Great Yankees Chaser," managing the Cleveland Indians, ca. 1954. *Courtesy National Baseball Library, Cooperstown, New York.*

threw the ball jerked the hell out of his arm and it caused him to come up with chips in his elbow. Lemon was a workhorse who could pitch a lot.

We had great pitching in Cleveland, no question. But I think the finest young prospect I ever saw come from school and then on up to the big leagues was Herb Score. He came up in 1952 and they brought him to Cleveland. They signed him right out of high school, Lake Worth High I think. Lake Worth is over by Palm Beach. They put a Cleveland uniform on him and took some pictures, stuff like that. The front office folks told him to loosen up and be ready to throw a few by the time I came over. Well, Score says fine and goes to it. Birdie Tebbetts was on the club at the time, maybe the last year he played, and he was warming him up.

When I finally came out they introduced me to him and we shook hands and I asked him if he had been throwing too long. I told him that if he had, we could wait until the next day. He says, "No, no, I've just been getting loose." So I asked him if he'd mind throwing a few hard ones. Well, Score turns and says, "Mr. Tebbetts, I'm going to let out." Tebbetts asks him, "You haven't been throwing hard yet?" Herb says, "No, not yet." So, Tebbetts said, "Hold on a minute." Then he calls in Joe Tipton, the other catcher. Tipton was kind of a screwball. "Hey Tipton, come here, I want you to catch this kid," Tebbetts yelled. Tipton comes over and, using Tebbetts' glove, says, "OK, kid." Score fired that first pitch and it just missed Tipton's head, went *swiiish.* It scared the hell out of Tipton. He didn't even get the glove up before the pitch hit the backstop. Tipton yells, "Tebbetts, you son of a bitch, you trying to get me killed!" So then he gets down in position to get his hands up faster. Score hit him on the foot with the next one. We had to get Jim Hegan to catch him.

After that we sent Score down to the minors. I think we sent him to Reading. His trouble was control. Herb Score was wild but what an arm. The Yankees had first crack at him but they turned him down because they never thought he would get the ball over the plate. After Reading he went to Indianapolis and had a great year. That was 1954, the year I had by far the best pitching staff in baseball: Early Wynn, Bob Lemon, Mike Garcia and Art Houtteman. In the bullpen I had Narleski, Mossi and Hal Newhouser. Tremendous pitching, the best I ever saw; Four Hall of Famers on that staff counting Bob Feller and Harold Newhouser.

That year, Score was having an outstanding year, voted the best minor league player in the whole country. Hank Greenberg, the Cleveland general manager says to me, "Hey, I got a good player for you." I asked him who. He says, "Herb Score." I say, "Herb Score? I don't need any pitching, Hank! I got the best pitching staff in the world. Get me an outfielder." I told him to let the kid stay down and finish the year and then next year we will give him a shot in spring training at Tucson. I said that in the spring, at Tucson, Arizona, first game we have, Herb Score is going to be the pitcher. Bring the kid up slowly, gradually, not in the middle of a pennant race. Why put the pressure on him? As I said, the problem with Score was control; he got nervous, wild, we could have broken his confidence. So he stayed down and had a great year and the next season he came up and was voted rookie of the year. He won sixteen games or so and led the league in strikeouts.

I wasn't still with Cleveland when Score was hit in the eye by the Gil McDougald line drive. I wish I had been there for him. I don't think that I would have tried to bring him back so fast. When he got hit in the eye, he was the star pitcher on the club. The big star on the team, really. Naturally there was a lot of pressure on the kid to get back in there. Score gets hit on the eye, and he was on medication because they were afraid of an infection in the eye. But, he came back too soon and by doing so he pulled his arm in Washington, D.C., and was never the same. He was built like a racehorse with real thin lines and his arm was as loose as it could be. He held the ball right on the tip of his fingers.

Vic Wertz was a guy that I enjoyed having on my team in Cleveland. He always found a way to help you win. I think Greenberg claimed him on waivers from the St. Louis Browns on account of his hitting. Greenberg was a great guy to have as your general manager. If he saw someone out there who could hit, he bought them. Wertz didn't field a lot, but Greenberg wanted him on the club. I was more in favor of fielding. Well, we are going to Boston in 1954 and all my big hitters are out of the lineup, hurt. Rosen had been hit in the face. Doby was hurt. I say jeez, I got to get some power in the lineup. So I called Wertz into my office and asked him if he'd ever played first base. He said, "Two games at spring training." I asked, what happened? He was playing for Fred Hutchinson at the time. He says, "I dropped a foul pop fly and Fred wouldn't let me play first no more." I said, "You're an outfielder and you missed the thing you should have caught, a pop fly." Well, when I asked him if he wanted to try it again he said he would. So, by God, I got him a glove and he played first base. Wertz won all four games for us in that series. He hit balls all over the ballpark. From then on I used him at first base and he became fairly acquainted with it. I used to take him out of the game around the seventh or eighth inning and put Bill Glynn or somebody else in for defense, but he was a great help. Vic Wertz really helped us at Cleveland.

We were blessed at Chicago to have one of the strongest middle infields around with Luis Aparicio at shortstop and Nelson Fox at second base. I mean, you couldn't beat having those two out there. They were both real fine ballplayers. Nellie Fox won the Most Valuable Player award with us in 1959. He used to use this big, thick-handled bat to spray the ball around and he could sure do it. That bat was a Roger Cramer model. Roger Cramer was the old center fielder for the Philadelphia Athletics and Nellie's bat used to be his model. When Nellie first came over to Chicago, he was a first baseman. Then Joe Gordon got to work on him at second base and taught him a lot, while Roger Cramer introduced him to that thick-handled bat so he would cut his swing down and spray the ball around the field more. It worked because Nellie became a great ballplayer.

I'll tell you a funny story about Nellie Fox. In those days club owners were baseball people and they all knew each other. Connie Mack had Nellie in Philadelphia. He had brought him up to the majors from Harrisburg, I think. Anyway, Mr. Mack had him on the club to play first base. Well, Nellie had no power and a first baseman has got to have power, so Connie Mack put him on waivers. Back then the waiver price was $15,000 or something like that and Clark Griffith from Washington claimed him. So Mr. Mack, thinking he was doing him a favor, called Griffith on the phone and said, "Mr. Griffith, I see where you claimed this young man Fox."

"Mr. Mack," Griffith says, "I need players. I'll claim a guy with one arm or one leg if I have to but I need players." Mr. Mack says, "Mr. Griffith, you're throwing your money away. Fox is not worth $15,000." So, Griffith withdrew the waivers and Mack kept him. Well, Nellie is on the club, and Chicago has got a guy by the name of Tipton, that screwball catcher I told you about, and he is not getting along with the manager, Jack Onslow. So Chicago wants to get Tipton off the club and they call Mack and Mr. Mack says, "I'll give you Fox for him." Chicago took him just like that, without finding out anything about him. I'd say Chicago got the better end of that deal. They shipped Tipton the hell out of there. By God, Nellie came over and between Joe Gordon helping on his fielding, making the double plays and stuff like that, and Roger Cramer with the heavy bat trying to hit the ball all over, they made him a good ballplayer.

You know, I am asked often how I think I would do managing today's ballplayers. I think I could handle the players of today; if you respect them then they'll respect you, whether they are big stars or not. I managed some great players. To me, they were not any better than anyone else on the team. You all had to work together. If you are not winning, you are going to have to change some spots. There are no superstars as far as I'm concerned. I played with some great players. But you go out there and try to win and don't worry about being a superstar; everyone is on the team.

At Cleveland, Bob Feller was, no question, a superstar, but he was getting older. He went 13–3, I think, in 1954, which was great. That's the kind of pitcher you want for a fifth or sixth guy. A veteran who can come in and go 13–3 is a real bonus. In 1954 he had some quality starts for us but in the World Series I had to bypass him in the fourth game and go with Lemon. Regardless of his record that season and the fact that he had won some games for us, he wasn't on par with the other pitchers we had. If he had still been great I would have been pitching him more regularly than for him to just go 13 and 3. Art Houtteman won 15 games in 1954. I would have gone to him before Feller. Bob Lemon was coming off three days' rest. I wanted to give him an extra day but I couldn't, I had to try to bring back my best pitcher. He pitched in New York the first day, then I pitched Wynn, then there was an off day, and then I pitched Mike Garcia and Lemon came back the fourth day.

As far as that 1954 World Series went, the Giants just played great ball. They made some great plays. Hank Thompson, the third baseman, played great and their pinch hitter, Dusty Rhodes, every time he went up he got hits or home runs. I guess the play everyone remembers though is the catch by Willie Mays of Vic Wertz's drive to center.

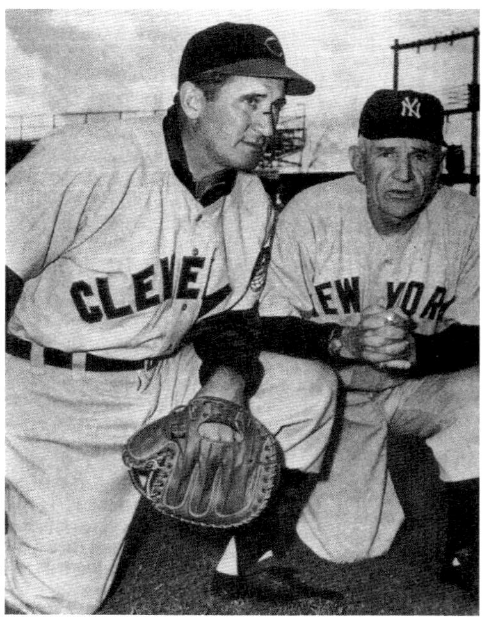

Lopez with Casey Stengel, manager of the New York Yankees, ca. 1954. *Courtesy Al Lopez.*

It was a great catch, no doubt about it. But, I think Mays overran the ball a little bit. He let it get over his head, but then he made the great play. That's the most difficult ball to catch, the one hit right over your head. He was coming from this angle and then the ball just got over his head. After the catch, the play became more sensational because of the way he turned and threw and then fell down. Still, a great play.

Vic Wertz was great for us in that series. He killed the ball that Mays caught. But with that deep center field, it had nowhere to go and Mays ran it down. Let me say this about the 1954 World Series. Our team won 111 games that year. That is still the record. I don't think we ever lost over 2 games in a row. Check it if you want. We never had a slump all year, you know. There hasn't been any club that ever played baseball that didn't have a slump during a season. I think that is what happened to us. We hit a slump at the World Series. The last three or four days of the season, I could feel the club was going down a little bit. Things were not going the way they should. We had clinched the pennant real quick and that might have hurt us.

The hitting kind of came apart for us; Doby and Rosen couldn't get it going. First man up, Al Smith, hits a home run. I think gee, that's great. But then Hegan hit a ball in the Polo Grounds that everybody thought was top tier. But the wind was blowing in and it blew the ball back. Monte Irvin, who made the catch, later told Hegan that the ball couldn't have missed the stands by an inch. It would have been a home run with three men on. Irvin said, "I gave up on it. I lost it in the stands, but then it came out." The upper tier in the Polo Grounds used to come out toward the field and Irvin said that the ball was up near the stands but started coming out and came down missing the stands not by an inch. That is the kind of stuff that went on. This was one of those series where I personally felt that the best team did not win. I think so on account of our pitching. We had great pitching. We should have won it. I think we were the favorite but it didn't happen.

That kind of stuff happens in the World Series. You watch the World Series year in and year out and you will find that there is always one or two guys that you don't expect to do any trouble that come through for their team. The stars never hurt you that much because, I guess, you concentrate more on those guys. In 1959, we'd never heard too much of Larry Sherry. We never heard of him and he came up and by God he was striking everybody out. They had a guy who played second base by the name of Charlie Neal. Neal played tremendous against us. He hit everything. Our report was that Johnny Roseboro, their catcher, had a strong arm but was a little erratic. We had a good running ball club but every time somebody tried to run, he made a perfect throw to get him.

I don't feel that there was anything different that I could have done to change the outcome of those two series. I always try to give the best I got. Try to work percentages and I don't think there was anything that I could do. After the 1959 season was over, Ty Cobb wrote me a real nice letter, I think it was the last one he wrote, congratulating me

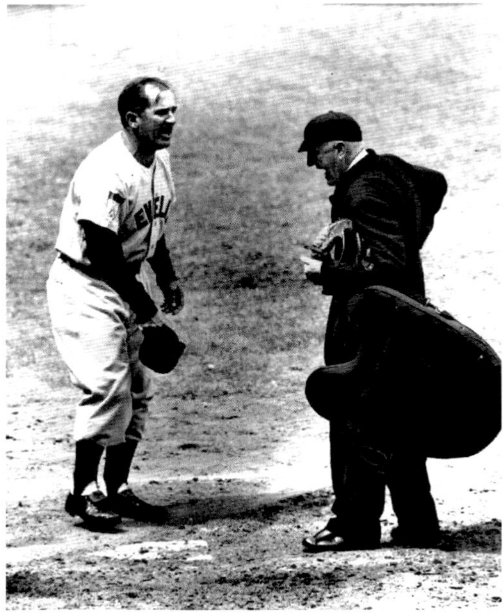

Lopez arguing a call with American League umpire Bill Grieve, June 23, 1951. *Courtesy UPI/Corbis-Bettmann.*

on managing the way I did, the old fashioned way. He claimed that is how they managed in the old days, scrap for a run, bunt, steal. We had to; we didn't have much power on the club. Sherm Lollar and Kluszewski helped; I could switch the two in and out. Jim Landis did a great job for us. He came out of nowhere and played great center field.

There was a pitcher on the Yankees who really had it in for Landis. The guy wore these big, thick glasses. A relief pitcher, he could throw hard. For some reason he used to knock poor Landis flat on his back every time. What the hell was the pitcher's name? He finally knocked Landis down in spring training, in St. Petersburg, the following year. Knocked him down in spring training! I say, Holy Jesus, here Landis is on the ground, and I went out and asked him if he was all right because it burned me up. It burns you up when they throw at your guys during the season, but in spring training, my God! What the hell was the name of that goofy guy?

Anyway, I told Yogi, I gave him a warning. I said you tell him the next time he throws at Landis, I'm going to get somebody in there when he comes up to hit, because pitchers hit in those days. There was no designated hitter then. I guess Yogi must have told him. Well, after we got to Chicago, the Yankees came in for an early season series. Back then, the east came west to start the year. In the middle of the game, Stengel, who was the manager, brings him in. Duren, Ryne Duren was his name. The first time Landis comes up to face him, Duren throws at him again. And they were beating us, I think! Yeah, they were beating us about 7–1. By God, I called the bullpen and told them to get me someone who will drill him in the ribs. I didn't want to throw at his head because Duren wore glasses.

The only volunteer was a Cuban boy, name of Arias, Rodolfo Arias. He volunteered right off. Sure enough, I talked to him in Spanish, he couldn't speak English. He was a left-handed sinkerball pitcher and I had wanted a sinkerball pitcher because the sinker hurt more. So I told him to go ahead and to throw the first pitch outside before coming into the ribs. I told him not to throw at his head though. I wanted the first pitch outside so he isn't suspicious. The first pitch he might have been thinking about it. Well, the next pitch Arias came inside and meant to hit him but missed and Duren jumps back, you know. I guess it must have dawned on him, because he looks at the dugout and I yelled, "Yeah, you God dammed right, we're gonna getcha." The next pitch hit him on the hipbone and Duren looked at Arias and hollered, "You son of a bitch, wait 'till you come up." But I yelled from the dugout, "You ain't gonna get him because I'm going to take him out."

Tony LaRussa and Lou Piniella are two managers who are doing a fantastic job. Lou did a great job with Cincinnati and I think that Tony has done a great job wherever he has been. Tony and his pitching coach, Duncan, I think, did a remarkable job with the pitching at Oakland and now in St. Louis. They took pitchers that nobody else wanted and they made great pitchers out of them. The relief pitcher, Dennis Eckersley, he was with Cleveland and Boston as a starter; they make him a reliever and he winds up in the Hall of Fame. Tony has done a remarkable job. And I think that Lou has done a great job

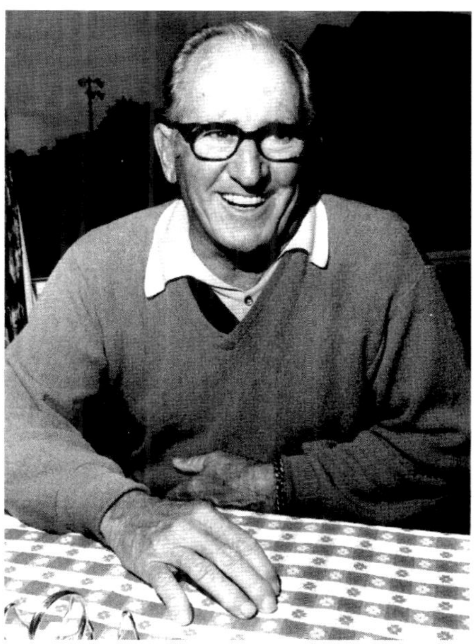

Al Lopez upon learning of his induction to the Baseball Hall of Fame, 1977. *Courtesy the* Tampa Tribune.

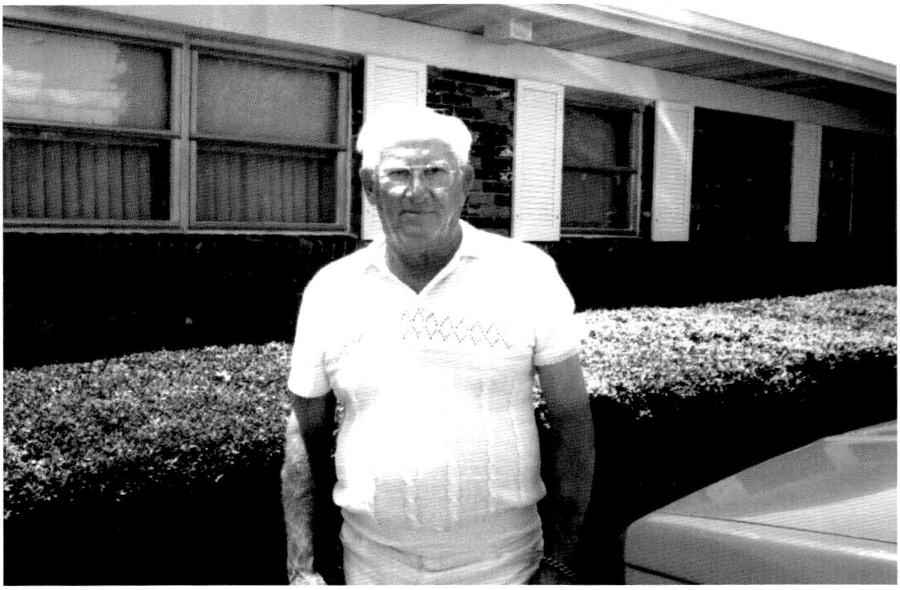

El Señor at home in Tampa, Florida, 1992. *Photo by author.*

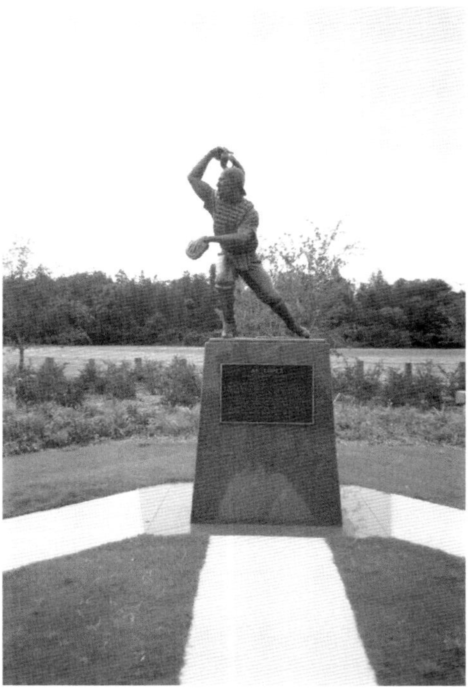

The Al Lopez monument, commissioned by the "Friends of Al Lopez Committee," Al Lopez Park, Tampa, 1992. *Photo by author.*

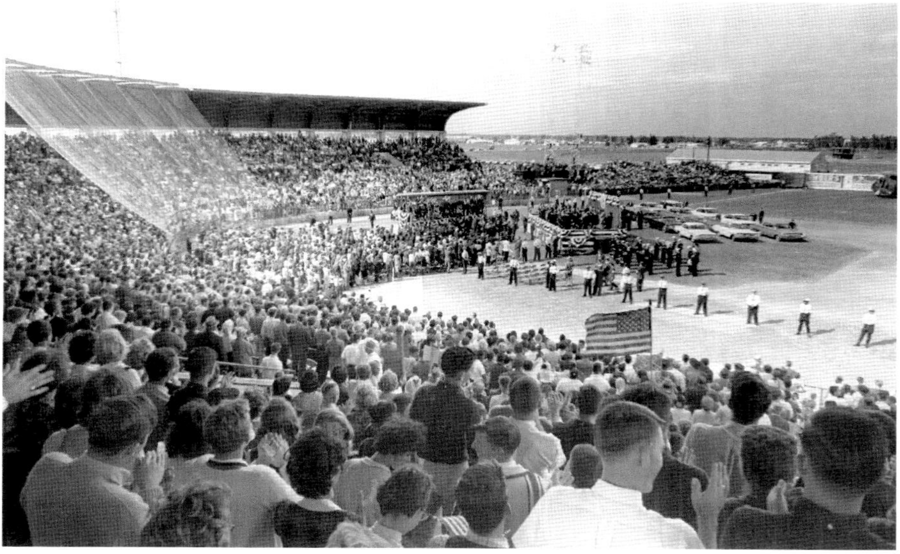

President John F. Kennedy speaks before a capacity crowd at Al Lopez Field, Tampa, Florida, November 18, 1963. *Courtesy Florida State Archives.*

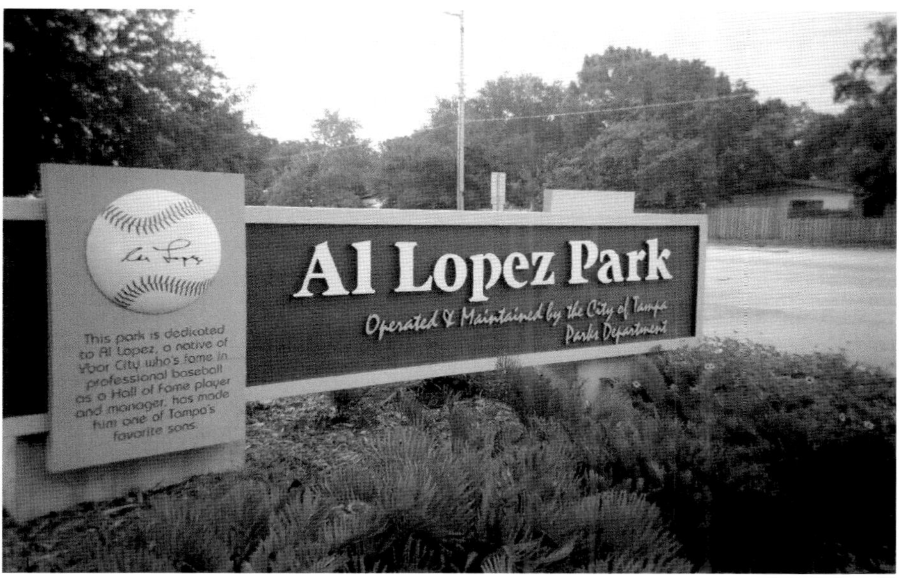

Al Lopez Park, Tampa, Florida. *Photo by author.*

as well. The only thing that I have been afraid for Lou has been his temper. Yeah, Lou's got a temper, but he's doing pretty good. Once in a while he blows up and picks up the first base bag and throws it at the umpire, but he does a real good job.

Did I tell you that I played under five Hall of Fame managers? Wilbert Robinson is a Hall of Famer. Max Carey is a Hall of Famer. He went in as a ballplayer though. Casey Stengel followed him. I played for Casey twice. Then I had Frank Frisch at Pittsburgh. He went in as a player. And then I had Lou Boudreau at Cleveland and he went in as a player. Those are all Hall of Famers. Did I mention Bill McKechnie? He is a Hall of Famer too, so that makes six Hall of Famers that I played for. I think that Robinson, Stengel, McKechnie and I went in as managers and the other fellows went in as players. I told that to what's his name, Mel Allen, at Cooperstown, and he couldn't believe it. He couldn't get over it. "My God, that's amazing," he said. He had me repeat that thing to three or four different people. "Hey Al, come here and tell 'em."

Today, I like to see St. Louis play. They do a lot of running and good fielding. That's the kind of ball they should play, because it's a big ballpark. It's not a home run ballpark. The Cubs, I like to watch the Cubs. Wrigley Field is an exciting ballpark. The Cubs don't steal that much. I'm glad to see they are getting good pitching right now. They're coming up with guys that are pitching like hell. You look at them and say, "Where did they get that guy from?"

Tampa has become a great place to find ballplayers and I feel very proud of that. Now the Major League team is in St. Petersburg. I don't want to knock St. Petersburg. You have to give them credit for going out and hustling up a franchise. But I think that the best location is still here in Tampa. This is the centrally located real estate. We are the flagship community and this is where they should have put a Major League ball club.

I want to say something about kids playing Little League baseball, American Legion baseball, scout ball—whatever you call it. I think it's great for kids to be able to go out and play baseball, especially for the little kids, ten, twelve, fourteen, fifteen years old. It's a great program and I have to give the coaches and the people who take time out to work with those kids a lot of credit. I think they have done a great job.

Here in Tampa, we have two kids—not kids anymore—who are managers in the Major Leagues and managed in the World Series against each other. That's amazing! Tony LaRussa when he was with Oakland against Lou Piniella when he was in Cincinnati. I don't think it's happened before in the history of baseball, two guys from the same town managing against each other in the World Series. Young guys that grew up together, one was from Ybor City and the other from West Tampa, but they played American Legion ball together. That was amazing. These baseball programs for kids are a good thing. Now if they could just keep the parks. They tore down Al Lopez Field, and I don't care because it was named after me, but because they shouldn't be tearing down ballparks. The kids need a place to play. But they are doing nice things around here; there is no doubt about it.

Russell Mallory Scarritt

> I don't have much stuff from my playing days. My house burned down on Christmas Day right after I quit playing and burned everything I had saved. It's all gone for the most part. People remember me though.
>
> —Russ Scarritt

During his 1929 rookie season, Russ Scarritt set the Boston Red Sox record for most triples in a season with seventeen. This mark also equaled the live-ball-era league record for rookies set by Charlie Gehringer in 1926. Scarritt was the regular left fielder for the Red Sox that year, batting a healthy .294. He also displayed a deft ability at manning "Duffy's Cliff," an incline at the base of Fenway Park's famed left field wall. Scarritt followed that up with a 1930 sophomore season in which he batted .289 over 113 games played.

Due to some minor injuries, however, Scarritt's playing time was reduced by about 25 percent that season. Taken with his wife's terminal illness—she was dying from cancer—Scarritt proved to be tremendously distracted. After the death of his wife, the torch Scarritt once held for the game went out. He finished his brief career playing for the Phillies in 1932, and after trying his hand in Texas oil wells, decided that he'd had enough and returned home to Pensacola, Florida.

I was born and grew up in Pensacola, Florida. My family on my mother's side was early settlers into the area. I played sandlot baseball growing up and, yeah, there was some talent around here then. There were quite a few good ballplayers in Pensacola. I never played any high school or American Legion baseball. I went to a military institute or prep school and didn't play there. Then I went to the University of Florida for a year and didn't play there either. I just wasn't playing much baseball at that time.

I didn't intend to play professional baseball at all. I had hoped to go to West Point and have a military career. I was supposed to get an appointment there but somebody with a little more pull than I had beat me to it. After they turned me down, I was offered an appointment to the coast guard academy but I told them to shove it. I'd wanted to go to West Point.

Well after that, this old fellow named Jack Ryan approached me about going off with him to play professional baseball. At first I said no but then I decided that I might as well try it. I had been playing some ball for the T.R. Miller Company of Brewton, Alabama, and that is where Ryan knew me from. The Miller Company had a team—there wasn't any money involved, but I had played for them. Ryan had wanted to get back into baseball and he had an offer from Johnson City, Tennessee, to come up and run the club and to pitch a little. Ryan was crafty; he would put tacks in his belt whenever he pitched to scuff the ball with. Well, I went with him and that was my first professional baseball, there at Johnson City, Tennessee. I was already twenty-three years old so I was starting a little late.

I wasn't too hot there those first years, I don't think. That was 1923 and 1924. Then I went on to Greenville, South Carolina, in the Sally League [South Atlantic League] and I had a lot better time of it. I hit .373 and set the league record for most number of hits in a season. That was a good Class A league with a lot of talent. I also led the league in RBIs. After two years in the Sally League I was sent to St. Paul, Minnesota, for Triple-A ball, one notch from the Majors. St. Paul was a long ways from Florida, it still is. I stayed another two years in St. Paul before Boston bought my contract and called me up.

Now, I don't remember what the deal was with my going to Boston because the Cubs were trying to get me too. I just think that St. Paul probably got a little more money from the Red Sox. In those days you took a train if you went anywhere, and that is how I traveled to Boston, by train. Boston seemed big to me after having been in St. Paul, Greenville and Johnson City. Then I got to Fenway Park for the first time and since I was being shifted from right field to left field I had to get used to playing "Duffy's Cliff." Duffy's Cliff was this hill in the outfield, about ten feet high, that led up to a walkway running along the fence from the left-field foul line to the center-field flag pole, and you had to run up that hill to field grounders because they would stay on top and not roll off. Sometimes I would run halfway up it and fall down. I'd get up and have to finish running up there. That was something else. Later on they cut the hill down and you just had that wall, the "Green Monster," but at that time you had the hill to deal with too. Duffy's Cliff was named after Duffy Lewis, who had played left field when Tris Speaker was in center and Harry Hooper in right. That was one of the greatest outfields of all time.

I got to Boston in 1929 and they were a bad team. I guess the problem was they just needed some good ballplayers. One of my teammates was a guy named Elliot

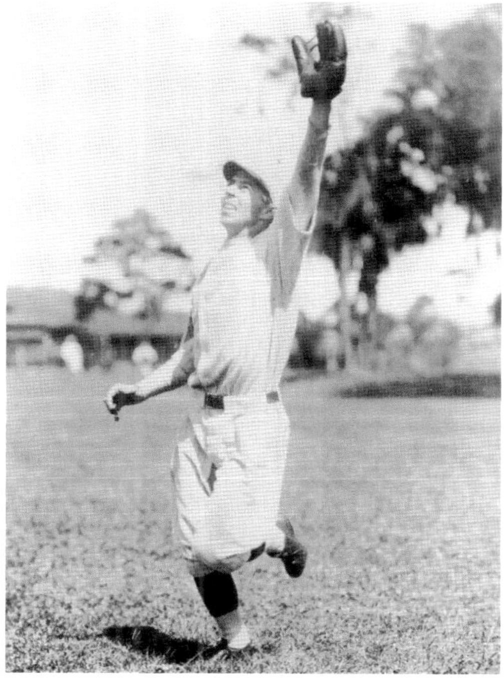

Scarritt readies himself for "Duffy's Cliff," 1929. *Courtesy National Baseball Library, Cooperstown, New York.*

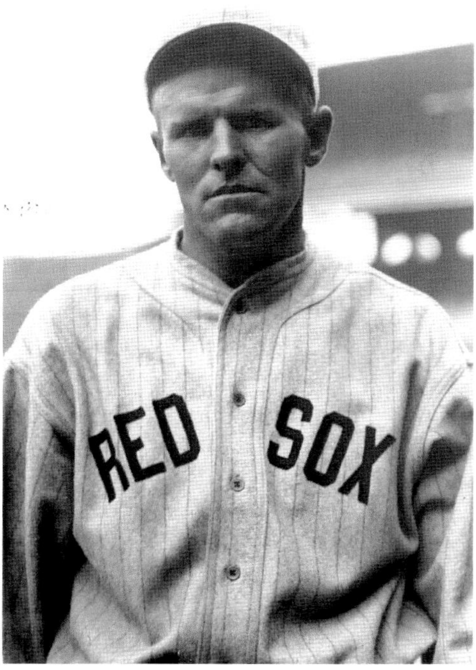

Elliot "Babe" Bigelow. *Courtesy National Baseball Library, Cooperstown, New York.*

Bigelow from Tarpon Springs, Florida. He got to Boston the same day that I did, came up from Greenville. It was amazing, two Florida guys showing up like that at the same time. Bigelow was a good hitter but wasn't much in the field, slow. Bigelow was a bit of a character though. He died young, down in Tampa I think.

Red Ruffing was a good right-handed pitcher on that Boston team but didn't have much success. He found his success later on with the New York Yankees. Tom Oliver was a good outfielder from Montgomery, Alabama. Hit the ball real well. Jack Rothrock was another good ballplayer on that team. Phil Todt was the first baseman on the team and he was a very good first baseman too. Todt could hit; he was an all-around good player. Earl Webb had a very good year in 1931, led the league in doubles, but I've lost track of him and don't know what ever happened to him.

The fans in Boston treated me all right. You might think that a last-place team wouldn't draw, but they turned out pretty good. They talked a lot about all the great players that had been sold out of there—Babe Ruth, Carl Mays and others. I don't think that they ever got over that. They liked me all right though. Maybe it was because I led the league in triples my first year—American and National League. It's an exciting play. I got all those triples just by legging it. I hit the ball to all fields, taking advantage of the corners. But the reason for the triples was that I was fast. In a full baseball uniform, with spikes and sliding pads and starting from the crossover step, I could run the hundred-yard dash

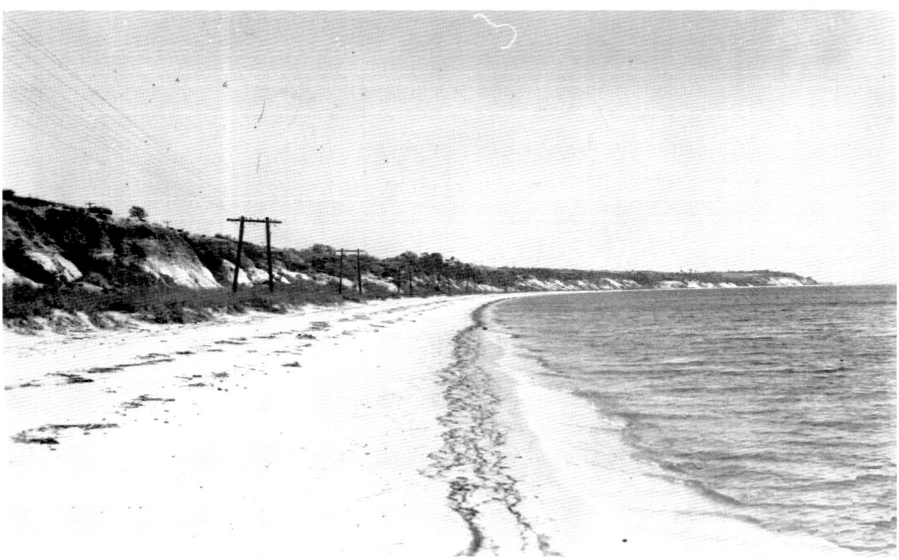

"I got all that speed from chasing those 'John Henry' crabs down there in Escambia Bay." Escambia Bay, Pensacola, Florida. *Courtesy Florida State Archives.*

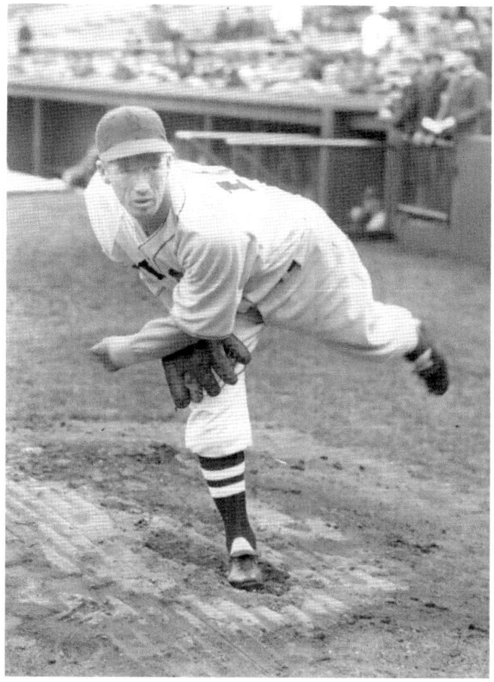

Robert Moses "Lefty" Grove, Boston Red Sox. *Courtesy National Baseball Library, Cooperstown, New York.*

in ten seconds flat. I would have been faster without all of the gear. But they didn't let us run a whole lot in Boston. I could run more in the minor leagues. I think I got all that speed from chasing those "John Henry" crabs down there in Escambia Bay when I was growing up. You spend all day running in knee-high water and it gave you leg strength.

I went to Cuba to play ball on an exhibition tour with an all-star team in 1930. Dizzy Dean and Chuck Klein were two of my teammates. What will surprise you is that the teams that we played against in Cuba were all Americans—there weren't any Cubans. A lot of black Americans were playing ball in Cuba and that's who we would play. A guy that owned the brewery in Cuba, Cervéza Tropicále, put on the exhibition tour.

I hit the ball pretty good when I was in Boston. Before each game I would try to relax and think to myself that here was just another pitcher, except when Grove was out there. I faced Grove when he was with the Athletics. Lefty Grove could smoke it; just get that ball in there. Grove was the fastest pitcher that I ever saw, even faster than Walter Johnson. I saw them both and I think that Grove was the fastest. Johnson was getting a little older when I saw him, but Grove was faster.

George Earnshaw was a damn good pitcher. Many people don't talk about Earnshaw anymore but they should, he was damn good. Earnshaw was a big, tall guy; good arm. Jimmy Foxx was on that team too, a big hitter. Later on I heard that Jimmy Foxx went to pieces. He got into some bad times they tell me. Al Simmons, Mickey Cochrane—Mr. Mack had some good players.

New York and Boston were big rivals then, still are. The Yankees were hard to beat and we didn't beat them very much. Lou Gehrig was a gentleman and the finest player I ever saw, but Babe Ruth was rough. I used to talk with him sometimes in between innings and he used to say, "You count them and I'll hit them." Once, I was playing right field in Yankee Stadium and when Ruth came to the plate I backed way up against the fence. I made a number of putouts against him that day. After one catch, when I was coming in and Ruth was going out, he says to me, "Say kid, why don't you come in and see the game." He was digging me about playing him so deep.

Bill Dickey was the catcher for the Yankees. It has been argued for quite a while about who was the better catcher, Bill Dickey or Mickey Cochrane. Personally, I guess I would have to stop and think about it. Bill Dickey caught me off second one time. I was playing a little too deep off second and he called for a pitchout and caught me off second base. I don't know that it was so much Dickey's arm as the fact that the play was all planned. I guess it's still up in the air over who was the better catcher.

I saw my share of good infielders too. Charlie Gehringer, Joe Cronin—they were all great. Leo Durocher played with the Yankees then and he wasn't much of a hitter but he was a hell of a shortstop. He used to really go get them. Heinie Wagner and Bill Carrigan, the two managers I played for in Boston, were both nice fellas. They would help you out the best they could. They just didn't have anything to work with. Heinie Wagner had been Bill Carrigan's assistant when Carrigan had won the World Series in 1915. Of course, they didn't have the same players back then.

It really didn't matter to me who it was I played against. I enjoyed myself and made some friends. Milt Gaston was a good friend and teammate of mine, a pitcher. He was from New Jersey. It was hard for me to keep a roommate; I had so much sickness to deal with. My wife had breast cancer and I had to stay home and take care of her. We had grown up together and she went through a great deal of pain with the cancer. We got married in 1923 and she died in early 1933. She'd had a hard time of it because she'd lost our first child and that threw her for a loop, and then she got the cancer. It took a lot out of me after she died and I just decided to quit baseball. You know, I didn't go on a date for four years after that.

In 1932, after not playing much the year before because of my wife's sickness and some minor injuries, I was traded to Philadelphia in the National League. In baseball you're just trading material, I guess. I couldn't understand why they traded me to Philadelphia. I still don't know why, I never found out. It just took me off my feet. After that, and with my wife being sick, I just went through the motions even though

I wasn't getting much of a chance to play anyway. My heart wasn't in it anymore. I was ready to call it a day.

I think that I would have done all right on a better ball club. I did pretty good on the ones I was on. After I got out of baseball they started getting fellas who if they got a scratch on them they would have to get a doctor to look at them and all that. In my day if the injury wasn't serious then you played. I think that the game has changed for the worse. They don't have to go through the minors like we did. They just throw that money around. It looks like they could give us some of it, but they don't do it. My top salary was only $6,000.

When my wife passed away and I left baseball, I plugged into oil prospecting out in Texas and dug a few dry holes, and finally gave up on it and had to go to work. I got a job with Ford Motor Company here in Pensacola as a service manager and worked for them for forty years. It kept me busy. My brother Francis had tried to get me to go in with him on a Lincoln-Mercury dealership in St. Petersburg, but I didn't want to leave Pensacola. He did pretty good for himself down there.

After I came back here, I played a little ball with the Class D Pensacola Flyers, with the understanding that I would get my release at the end of the year. Bob Kitchens was the manager and he agreed to it. I didn't really enjoy playing for them all that much, I just did it as a favor.

I don't watch much baseball on television; I never did. It used to make me edgy watching it. I like football though; I'm a big football fan. I like to watch college football but I never did play. I had an older brother, Jerry Scarritt, who died as a young man and who played football at Auburn and the University of Florida. He played football, baseball and ran track—an athlete. Jerry died down in Gainesville in 1904 of typhoid fever and pneumonia that he'd picked up from a contaminated well.

My house burned down on Christmas Day right after I quit playing, I lost all of my stuff that I had saved from my playing days; it burned everything I had. It's all gone for the most part. People remember me though. I get about three letters a week looking for autographs. I sign them and send them back. There is a club here in town where a band plays on Wednesday night and they used to introduce me to the customers and I would sign autographs for them. I signed 131 one day out in front of a store. I had to stop for a while and rest.

I really enjoyed playing baseball. I had a good time and I have no regrets. I would do it again without thinking about it. All these fellas now that used to play ball—eighty, eighty-five, and I'm ninety-one—we are getting up there in age but I'm feeling pretty good. They tell you now that you can't eat this and you can't eat that, well I eat whatever I damn well please, always have, always will.

Manuel Domingues "Curly" Onis

> I thought Manuel had possibilities. He had a good arm and was a tough guy. One of those rugged guys, you know, a catcher. I think he would have made it, but I think getting in trouble with the umpire hurt him.
>
> —Al Lopez, *Tampa Tribune*, July 15, 1993

Manuel Onis was a tough, strong-armed catcher who, in 1935, debuted with the Brooklyn Dodgers. A son of Spanish cigar makers and raised in Ybor City, Onis had been signed on the recommendation of his friend Al Lopez. He progressed rapidly through the minors to join Lopez, Casey Stengel and others in Brooklyn. Upon arriving there, Onis belted a single in his only at-bat prior to being sent back to the minors on a ten-hour recall. The anticipated recall never came and because of this, Onis remains the rare 1.000 lifetime batter.

I was born and raised near the corner of Seventeenth Avenue and Columbus Drive in Ybor City, Tampa, Florida. We played a lot of baseball on the sandlots back then; it's all we had to do. We didn't have a radio or television or anything so we played sandlot baseball. In front of our house was a sand street that had a streetcar running on it. You know, I have a funny story about the streetcar. When I was about six years old the streetcars would switch in front of our house and I used to take my little seat, a rocker, and would put it on the track and then sit on the porch and wait for the streetcar to come. When it did, it would have to stop and this fellow would get off and pick it up and put it back on the porch. I was six years old and I was trying to derail it!

My parents were originally from Spain; one from Asturias and the other was from Galicia. They left Spain, stopped in Cuba for a time and then came on in here and

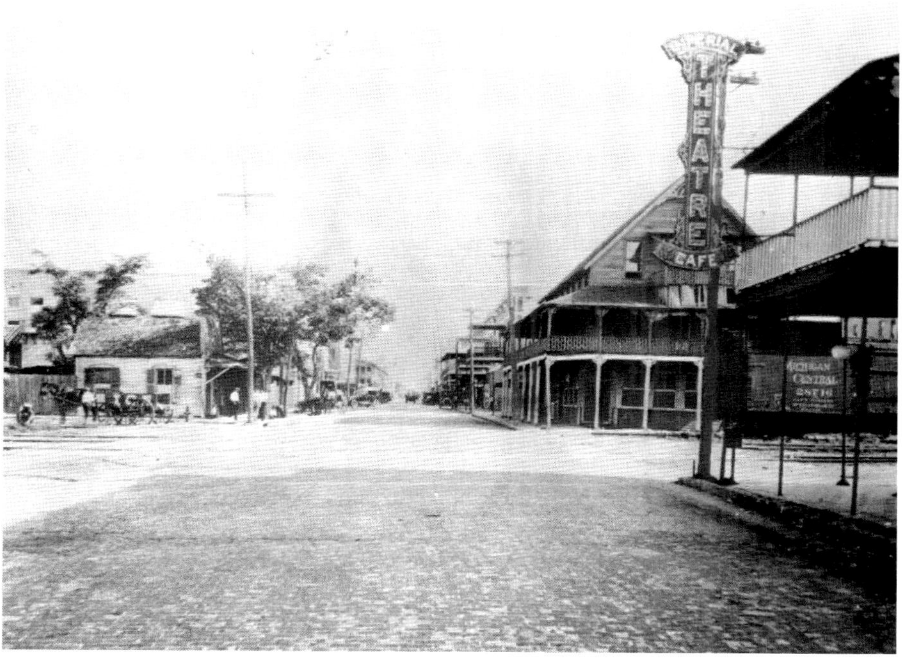

Ybor City street scene, 1910. *Courtesy Florida State Archives.*

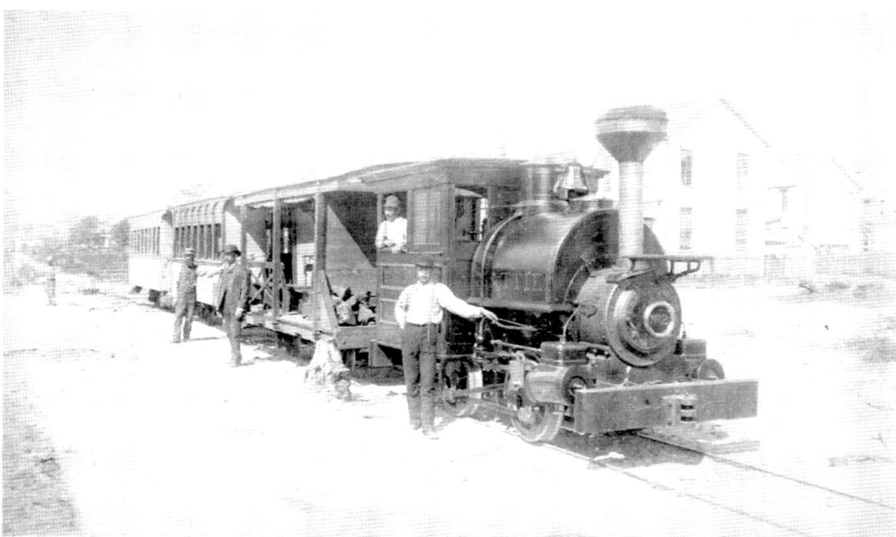

Tampa street railway "I was trying to derail it." *Courtesy Florida State Archives.*

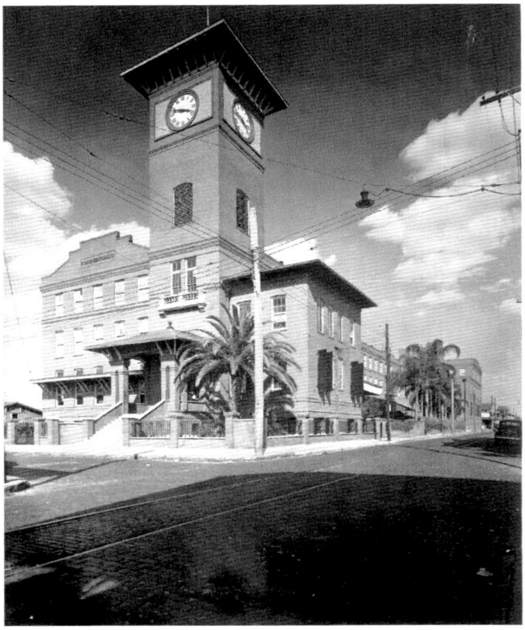

Regensburg Cigar Factory. *Courtesy Florida State Archives.*

went to work in the cigar factory. They worked over in the Regensburg factory on Columbus Drive and Sixteenth Street. We lived just a couple of blocks from there. I didn't go to high school; I went to George Washington Junior High. I started playing what you might call organized baseball in a city league here in Tampa.

In 1929 I had gone to work for the Tampa Electric Company. They gave me a job if I would catch for their baseball team. I went to catch but there weren't no jobs. But then, they got me a job running the streetcars; the same ones I wanted to derail. You know that I met the guy that used to pick the rocker up off the tracks and put it on my porch. His name was Ross; he was a German fellow, about six feet tall. Ross was still running the streetcars.

I played 1929 and 1930 in the city baseball league with the Tampa Electric Company. In 1931 Al Lopez, who was playing for Brooklyn and was also from Ybor City, recommended me to a friend of his that was a manager in Johnstown, Pennsylvania, and that manager took me with him. It was a minor league team but I have forgotten what class it was. I stayed there one year, caught one year there, and then they released me and I came back home.

Then I played here in Tampa with a team they called the Cuban Stars. In 1933, when I was with the Cuban Stars we went to New York on kind of a barnstorming exhibition tour. I saw that big city and was scared to death. We had a couple of guys on the team that could have played in the big leagues. We stayed up there about two months. We played against the black teams mostly. They had some real good ballplayers. Good ballplayers!

The following year I went into what they called the Georgia-Florida League. I was catching at the time, for Jacksonville, and I got a call from Al Lopez and he asked me, "Can you come up here?" I said sure; man I was excited! He said, "They want to look at you because I recommended you." Casey Stengel was the manager in Brooklyn at the time. So I said, "Well Al, I don't have no fare; I've got no money for the ticket." I didn't have it either. So Al sent me a ticket. Then I got on the train and went to New York and he met me at the railroad station. I had told Al to meet me at the station and he did and he took me in. Boy, I was really excited and the next day he took me to the ballpark. I can still close my eyes and see Ebbets Field; I was on top of the world, you know?

I stayed with Brooklyn for a month in 1934, although I didn't play, mostly bullpen duty, and then they sent me to Allentown, Pennsylvania. I finished out the season there and then went back to Brooklyn. Al had this little automobile and we drove it home to Tampa. I am telling you, that was some experience. All of the roads were rocky and dirt, hard driving, but we made it home. When we got there my friends all wanted to know how it was in Brooklyn with the Dodgers because none of them had ever been out of Tampa. We talked about it a lot. Al and I spent the winter playing golf in West Tampa. The city had a nine-hole golf course there. You only needed to use a driver, a putter and a wedge. That's all it took!

While I was in Tampa that winter, I got a telephone call from one of the directors in the Brooklyn office and he said, "Manuel, I'm sorry but I forgot to sign you up." They wanted me to go to spring training with them but I wasn't under a contract. So, they sent me a contract, I signed it and sent it back. When camp started we went to Orlando to train. I had a nice training session there. I hit .359 in sixteen ballgames and I caught most of them; I was ready. One game I caught was against the New York Yankees. Of course, they had some players. During the game, Lou Gehrig hit a screamer right back to the mound and the pitcher had to fall flat to avoid it. Gehrig hit it so hard; our center fielder caught it on a line.

While I was catching, Lopez was just messing around. He wasn't worried about making the club, losing his job or anything. Meanwhile I was working hard. Well anyway, the club liked me, so when camp ended they carried me up to Brooklyn with them.

Once there, the catchers were Al, Babe Phelps and me. After the season started, we were sitting there on the bench during one game, in about the seventh or eighth inning, and Stengel leaned over and he looked at me and asks, "You want to catch?" Of course, I told him that is what I was there for. He said, "Well go on in there." I

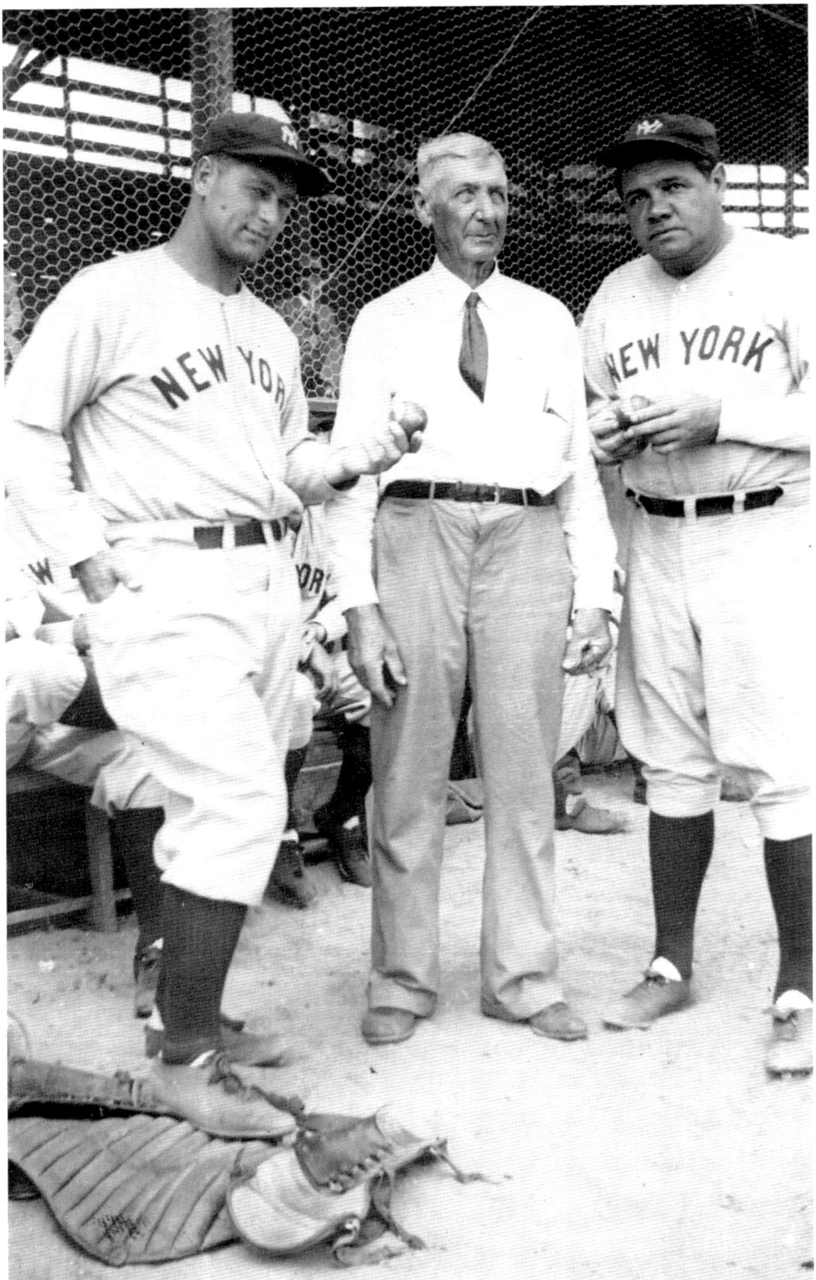

Lou Gehrig and Babe Ruth, spring training in Florida, 1934. *Courtesy Florida State Archives.*

went over and put my stuff on and man, I was shaking. I can't explain the feeling and you can't realize the feeling that I had at that time, when they told me to get in there.

Johnny Babich was pitching for us that day and we were playing Boston, then the Boston Braves. So I went in there to catch and do you know that the ground was still frozen when we started to play? There was ice on the field. We went ahead and played the inning out and went back to the dugout and my time came to bat. I went up there and I couldn't stand at the plate; I was so nervous. George Magerkurth was the umpire, stood about six foot two, a big, huge man. Lefty Brandt was pitching. Ed Brandt, a left-hander, one of the best that Boston had. He threw me a pitch and it was a strike. So I stepped out of the batter's box, stooped over to get some sand in my hands and Magerkurth stepped by me and he said, "Get up there and hit, son." Then he walked off, didn't even look at me or nothing, but I heard him. So that kind of gave me a little strength, you know? I turned back on the plate and this guy Ed Brandt threw me a curveball and I hit it right over the third baseman. Jeez, I ran to first base and I got there and couldn't get off the base. I didn't want to get picked off; I didn't know what to do. I stayed right there at first base; nobody could move me over. When I got the hit, Al told me that Casey turned to him and said, "Where did you get this guy?" Well, the inning ended, then I caught the ninth inning and that was it. I guess I thought there would be plenty of other chances.

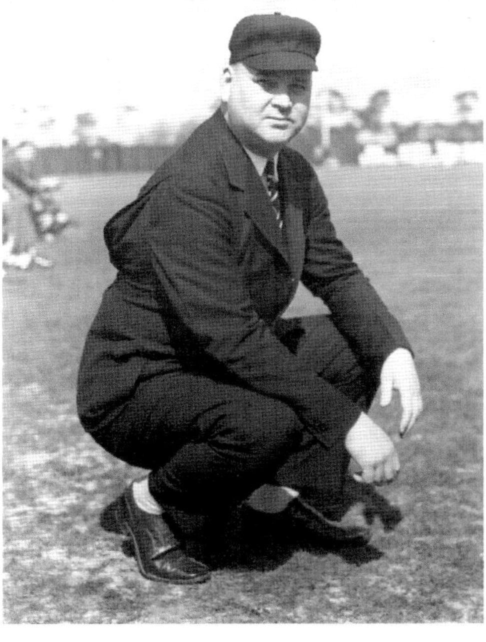

George L. Magerkurth, National League umpire, 1936. *Courtesy National Baseball Library, Cooperstown, New York.*

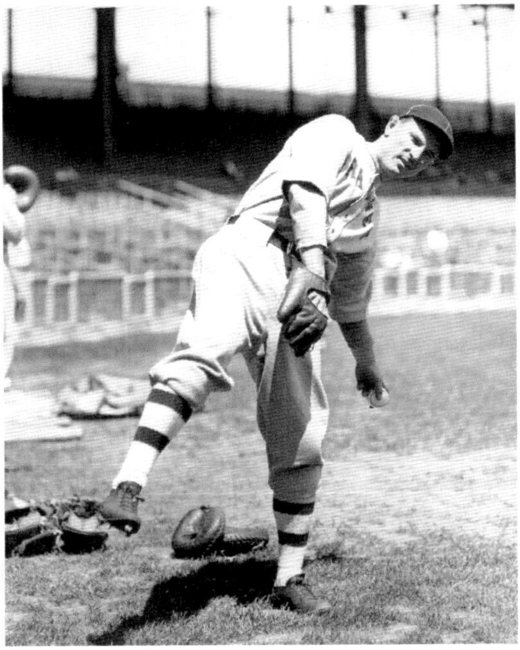

'Big Ed' Brandt, Boston Braves, 1931. *Courtesy National Baseball Library, Cooperstown, New York.*

I stayed there with Brooklyn until they had a cut-down of their roster but I didn't get any more at-bats. That was the only year that the Major Leagues cut the roster to twenty-four players. It's always been twenty-five, and I was the twenty-fifth. So, when the cutting date came they sent me to Dayton in the Mid-Atlantic League. Brooklyn had me on a ten-hour recall so I could come back if they needed me. But before I got back to Brooklyn, an incident occurred. We were playing in Wilkes-Barre, Pennsylvania, and we had lost four games in a row. Everybody was upset and so was I. We started the game and I stooped down to catch. Late in the game the first baseman for Wilkes-Barre came up to bat and we had him, two strikes and two balls. Then my pitcher threw a pitch that was right down the middle. I swear today that it was right down there and the ump called it a ball! Oh boy, that started it right then; I was steamed up about it. The next pitch, the guy hits a home run.

Well, you know how I felt and so I raised hell with the umpire. "I'm going to charge this ballgame to you," I kept arguing. He said, "Get down there and catch or I'm going to throw you out." I said, "If you throw me out I'm going to hit you on the head!" So he threw me out and I hit him on the head. I hit him with my catcher's mask and it cracked open his head, I guess, and he was bleeding there at home plate. I started pounding him with my fists, but they separated us and I was out of the game. The umpire was all right but I got suspended without pay for thirty days and fined $25. You can imagine; I was only making $150 a month to begin with and now on top of the fine I was suspended. The team sent me back to Brooklyn because the umpires wouldn't even let me stay on the field. Then after that, Brooklyn released me; I think they feared trouble with the umpires. My temper cost me a lot.

The next year or so I played in Fort Worth, Texas, and Sioux City, Iowa. Then in 1937 and 1938 I played for Leesburg, Florida, and after that Washington bought my contract, in 1939. Washington made me the player-manager of the club in Charlotte, North Carolina. At the end of the season in Charlotte I got a broken ligament in my knee. When I broke my knee I couldn't squat down anymore and I didn't have it repaired at the time as I should have. I told Washington that since I couldn't play I wasn't coming back. They tried to get me to come back. They said, "We'll fix your knee." I wasn't going back. By the way, it was Lou Klein who broke it. He ran into me at home plate; I had him by about ten feet and he ran into me with his legs up and hit me right on the knee.

Well I came back home and I had a friend at Tampa Electric who was the operator of the streetcars. I told him, "Mr. Sheridan, I can't play ball no more and I need a job." Jobs were hard to get. He said OK, he would put me on the streetcars for twenty-two cents an hour and I said fine. I worked there a little less than a year. I understood from the guy, however, that the streetcars were going to be taken off the

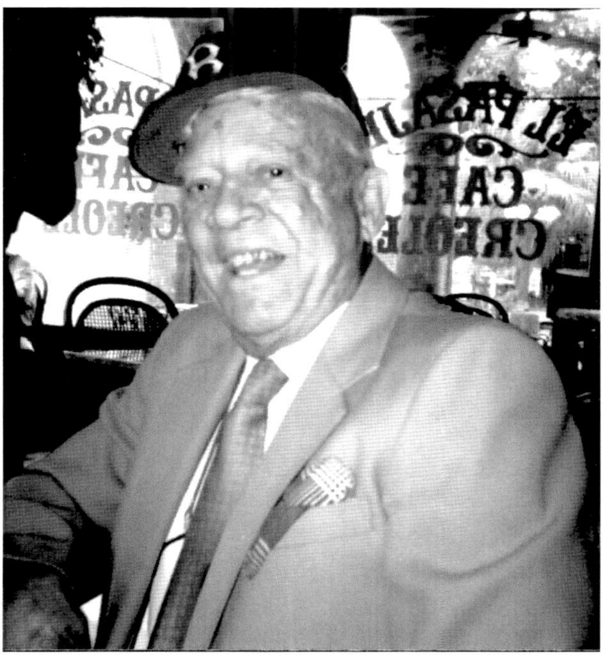

Manuel Onis at Café Creole, Ybor City, Florida, 1993. *Photo by author.*

line soon. They were going to be removed. Then the president of the Italian club, a guy who was the operator of a ball team, asked me to be his manager. I said that if he wanted me to manage then he was going to have to get me a job. He was a well-liked guy in the city, a lot of connections. He said OK, and we had a deal.

So after I had been with Tampa Electric about nine months, this guy calls me and said that they wanted me to report to the fire department. So I went and the fire chief was Mr. White and he was a tough customer. He carried a pistol right on his hip. Those were rough times around here. Chief White tells me to go to station Number 1. The next morning I got my boots and I went to Number 1 and I stayed there twenty years until I retired from the fire department and that was it.

Yes, there are regrets. Sometimes, I wake up wondering what I could've done with another chance in the Majors. I was good. I could throw and hit. There's no telling. Man, I'm sorry for hitting that umpire. I was such a hothead. Now I tell people, don't argue with umpires. You can't win.

Jimmy Bloodworth

When I was a kid, there were only two guys from Florida playing in the big leagues that I knew of, Al Lopez and Jimmy Bloodworth.

—James P. Jones, Florida State University, June 1990.

Jimmy Bloodworth, "The Pride of Apalachicola," began his eleven-year Major League career in 1937 with the Washington Senators. In a stretch that was interrupted by World War II, Bloodworth earned his stripes in stops at Detroit, Pittsburgh, Cincinnati and Philadelphia, proving to be a valuable glove man in the process. A member of the pennant-winning 1950 Philadelphia "Whiz Kids," Bloodworth maintained a slick .926 lifetime fielding percentage. Today, the baseball field at Apalachicola High School bears his name.

I grew up in both Eastpoint and Apalachicola, Florida. My grandparents lived in Eastpoint and I stayed with them all during the summer. I'd return home to Apalachicola and go to school during the winter. In Apalachicola, we would gang up and have baseball games all the time and that led up to high school, where I played ball competitively for the first time. By the time I graduated high school in 1937, I was already playing organized ball in Chattanooga, Tennessee.

I'd begun playing pro ball when I was a sophomore in high school, 1935, in Panama City [Florida]. Panama City had a Class D league team then and they needed some ballplayers so I signed on to play with them. That was probably around the middle of the year, and at the end of the season the Chattanooga ball club bought me. Chattanooga was a Washington Senators affiliate and I went to play for them at the end of Panama City's season. From 1937 until 1939 Washington kept me at Chattanooga to improve some before bringing me up to take a look and to see how I was progressing.

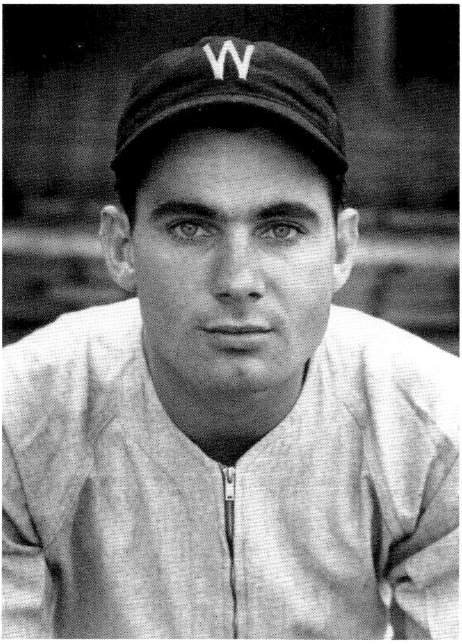

Jimmy Bloodworth with the Washington Senators. *Courtesy National Baseball Library, Cooperstown, New York.*

When I first got to Washington my tonsils were sunburned because my mouth hung open looking up at those buildings; I'd never seen anything like that before. I remember Wes and Rick Ferrell were on that ball club. Al Simmons was on it too. Simmons was one of the great right-hand hitters of all time. That was a terrific bunch of guys. People I'd read about my whole life; it was just about more than I could stand.

I was with the Washington club when we traveled to Yankee Stadium to play on July 4, 1939, Lou Gehrig Day. Haven't you ever seen the film of Gehrig giving his speech? It has become a famous scene. I tell you that was something; not a dry eye out there. The emotion in that place was unbelievable. And that 1927 Yankee team all standing over there alongside the 1939 Yankees; what players they had on both clubs—Babe Ruth, Bob Meusel, Tony Lazzeri, Frank Crosetti, Joe DiMaggio, Bill Dickey, what a group! We always played the Yankees tough into about the sixth or seventh inning but then they'd get some runs and run out the relief pitcher and that would be it.

Looking back, you'd have to say that I was a defensive player, glove man. My glove kept me up there. Anything I could get my hands on I figured I should catch it; regardless of a bad hop or how hard it was hit or anything. There were some great infielders back then. I was just thinking on the way over here that at the time that I was playing ball, Charlie Gehringer was second base for the Detroit Tigers, Bobby

Doer was second base for the Boston Red Sox, Joe Gordon played second for the New York Yankees, Johnny Beradino was the second baseman for the old St. Louis Browns and he later became a movie star. A manager could just about shut his eyes and pick a name and he'd have a pretty good second baseman. Of course Gehringer was the greatest second baseman I've ever seen. I was the first person who tried to replace him in Detroit and they are still looking for somebody to replace him.

The first time I ever went to bat in the big leagues was against Lefty Grove, who was then with the Boston Red Sox. I faced Grove when he was supposed to have been through, but he was still throwing aspirin tablets. I can't recall if I got a hit or not but Grove was something else; I remember that.

At the beginning of the war [WWII], Detroit was just like many of the other clubs then—they were missing Greenberg, we lost shortstop Billy Hitchcock—losing ballplayers all the time. I think we had three or four shortstops that first year of the war. I never knew who would be out there with me. It was a rough situation for all the ball clubs then. You just played whomever you could get.

Del Baker was our manager in Detroit. I also played for Bucky Harris over in Washington when I first went up, a great guy. Bucky Walters was the Reds manager when I came back after the war and went to Cincinnati. Then I went over to the

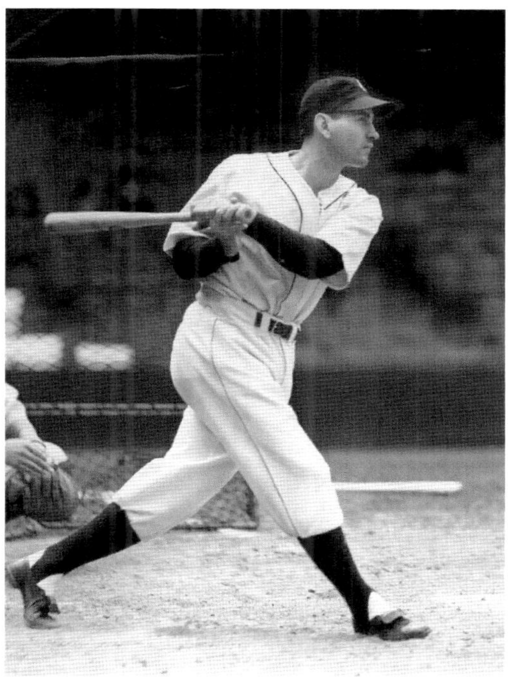

Charlie Gehringer, Detroit Tigers "They are still looking for someone to replace him." *Courtesy National Baseball Library, Cooperstown, New York.*

Philadelphia Phillies and Eddie Sawyer was the manager there. I think I played under some of the best managers that ever lived.

I was in the service in 1944, 1945 and part of 1946; the army engineers. I was stationed at Fort Leonard Wood, Missouri. I'd had formal National Guard training and just as soon as I went in I became an instructor and taught small arms weapons like the M1 rifle and Thompson sub-machine gun. Then I began teaching the bazooka, .50-caliber air-cooled and water-cooled machine guns and .30-caliber water-cooled and air-cooled machine guns. I also taught anti-aircraft firing with .50-caliber machine guns, and I taught mines. We had to learn all about the German mines and then we had to teach it. All the detonators, things like that. We had to know a whole lot about those mines, because if you didn't you would get a bunch of people killed. We were fortunate, thank God that we didn't get anyone killed during training. That is what I was doing.

I don't think the war had anything to do with my ball playing. I wasn't much of a ballplayer, wasn't a good hitter. I was a good fielder, I could hit a few home runs, I could hit a long fly ball to score a run from third, I could hit the ball to right field and I guess that kept me in a lot of ballgames. While in the service, we tried to put together a team at Fort Leonard Wood but we didn't get very far because that was a training company and every seventeen weeks there was movement. So, I didn't get much work during those years, but that was OK.

Ted Williams and Bob Feller are two prime examples of ballplayers whose careers were hurt by the war. Bob Feller lost over a hundred ballgames that he would have won. Ted Williams, you just don't realize what a hitter he was unless you did see him. Oh God, he was magnificent. Those people the war really hurt. Fellows like myself though, it didn't hurt us; I don't think so.

Because of the war, however, I missed the pennant in 1945 with Detroit. I just took that as my bad luck. But boy, I followed them while I was still in Missouri and I had radios and I was sneaking time to hear them and all; I was pulling for the Tigers. You know that Dizzy Trout and Harold Newhouser were good friends of mine. Those two ballplayers, they really pitched some great ball. In 1944 Newhouser won I think twenty-nine games and Trout won twenty-seven; that is fifty-six games between them that two ballplayers won. At one time I believe that Harold Newhouser was as great a left-handed pitcher as has ever been on that mound. He had everything you could work with and he used it. He knew how to pitch and he loved to pitch. I've seen him pitching out there on hot days; it's a wonder to me he lived as long as he did because he had a bad heart and his lips would turn blue, but he was still throwing that ballgame. Harold had a lot of intestinal fortitude. He is in the Hall of Fame.

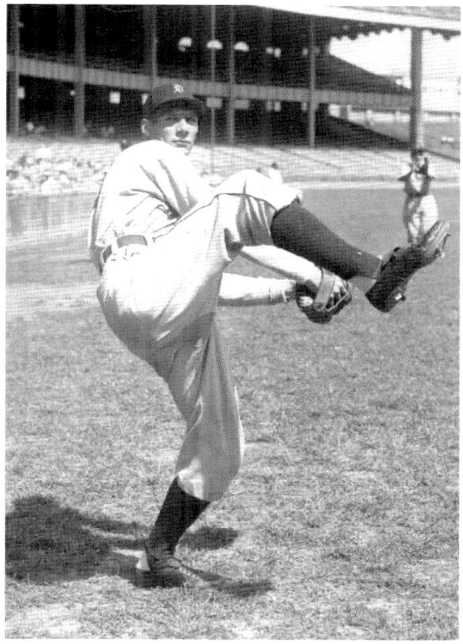

'Harold had a lot of intestinal fortitude.' Hal Newhouser, Detroit Tigers. *Courtesy National Baseball Library, Cooperstown, New York.*

At the end of the 1947 season I cracked my ankle, and so in 1948 Mr. Branch Rickey bought me. He was with the Dodgers then, and he sent me down to play in Montreal, Canada. During spring training he told me to get in good shape so that if they needed a veteran ballplayer, someone with experience, I would be it. That is what I was bought for. Montreal was their top farm club and was loaded with good young players. Both Roy Campanella and Don Newcombe were there. Campanella was the greatest catcher I've ever seen. Roy Campanella, what a gentleman. Brooklyn took him up in the middle of the season. Don Newcombe became a real pitcher there that season in Montreal. Chuck Conners was the first baseman and he went on to become an actor on television. I played second. A kid named Bob Morgan was the shortstop, and Duke Snider was our center fielder. Yes sir, Brooklyn had some good ones coming up. All real great kids too.

In 1950 I was traded to Philadelphia and enjoyed a really fun year. Playing with the "Whiz Kids" was a lot of fun. Every one of those young ballplayers, we had a bunch of youngsters, I'm talking about they were young ballplayers, and boy could they scrap. They were real scrappers.

When I first started playing in the big leagues, Al Lopez and myself were the only ballplayers from Florida up there that I knew about. It's a lot different today. We were the only two up there for a long time. When people would ask me where I was from I would say, "Apalachicola," and they would ask, "Where in the hell is that?" And I'd tell them,

"That's the home of the diamondback." "Mosquitoes and rattlesnakes will eat you up down there!" Then they would say, "I don't want to go there!" And I'd turn around, walk off and say to myself, "Good, because we don't want you either." But they found us. They're moving in on us so fast now it's about to make us want to move. And North Florida isn't so crowded yet like South Florida, but they're coming fast.

You know, it makes me feel so proud to think about all of the great ballplayers I met and played with both when I first came up and then the kids who came up after me; truly great players. I was mighty lucky to have stayed up there with them for twelve years.

I want to tell you something about Cecil Travis. He hit .359 one year and finished a mighty poor second in the batting race. Ted Williams hit .406 that 1941 season and beat him. Travis is another one that the war affected; it ended him. His feet froze during the Battle of the Bulge and he couldn't do anything, he had to call it quits. We had a good thing going there in 1941, him at shortstop and me at second. If we'd had more pitching we'd have been a good ball club. We scored a lot of runs. Dutch Leonard pitched for us that year and did a great job, won eighteen games; he had won twenty a couple of years earlier. He had a knuckle ball with great control and when he got his fastball and that rinky-dink curve over, he was tough to hit. Leonard was really a great pitcher.

As I said, Al Simmons, "Ole step in the bucket," one of the all-time greats, was at Washington when I arrived there. I'll tell you a little story about him. When he first got to the big leagues he went up to batting practice and he was stepping in the bucket as he always did. He played for Connie Mack and the Athletics. Connie Mack was manager there at Philadelphia, and Al Simmons stepped in the bucket and one of the coaches jumped up and said, "My God, we got to change that." But Mr. Mack, in his old calm way said, "Wait just a minute sir, let's see how Mr. Simmons does his way before we change him." They never bothered to change him and he had a lifetime batting average around .330 [.334].

Hank Greenberg was a teammate of mine in Detroit and again at Pittsburgh. He was a real gentleman. Greenberg was terrific; people didn't realize what a student of the game he was. He proved it because when he got through playing he went to Chicago as general manager and then to Cleveland and bought interest in the club. He was smart. He was a help to me both in baseball and financially.

I managed in Greenberg's baseball camp down in Daytona Beach, did it for three years. I had some of those bonus babies like Rocky Colavito and different ones. I saw Herb Score pitch, but he didn't come down to me. I was coaching B league and they couldn't send him to a B league because they couldn't pay a catcher enough money to go down there and catch him. It would have taken at least a Triple-A catcher to catch him.

There was nobody in spring training in Daytona Beach who could catch him either. The first two guys who tried, he threw that ball right on by them. The fellow they signed with Score, by the name of Dick Brown, was a catcher who caught Score in high school. I had him on my ball club then and also had the pleasure of recommending him for the big leagues. After Brown went to Cleveland, some Baltimore scouts talked to me and I told them what a prospect I thought he was and Baltimore got him in a trade. Brown became a top-notch catcher on that Baltimore club. Yeah, I was proud of him.

Ralph Kiner was another teammate of mine at Pittsburgh and I threw him batting practice on many a day. He was a great long-ball hitter, fifty-one homers one year. After Hank Greenberg came over we'd stay out at the ballpark after a game and Greenberg would help Kiner on hitting and I'd throw batting practice while another infielder would catch and we would get some of the ground crew to shag balls. But after we'd worked out for maybe a month, we didn't have to do much shagging because Kiner hit them all out of the ballpark.

Ted Kluszewski was another home-run hitter. He was a teammate of mine in Cincinnati. That was a big strong man. You can't realize; you would have to see him to believe it. He had those big arms hanging out of his shirt like that. He hit some balls so hard he would make them lopsided. He was also agile for a big man.

Robin Roberts, from the time I first met him, was always a gentleman. Easy going, quiet, but he'd get out there and pitch for you. Robin knew how to pitch too. He was always ready when you needed him. Richie Ashburn was a player and a real fun guy. Ashburn could get down that baseline about as fast as anyone you've ever seen. If he hit a ball two hops to an infielder, that infielder better get it on the way to first in a hurry because he'd beat it out. Ashburn could fly. That Phillies team seemed to lose its spark though the next year…I just don't know what happened. The 4–0 loss in the World Series in 1950 might have had something to do with it but I don't know. Those things happen in baseball. That spark was missing. Everybody on the club got along real good though, all nice fellows. Nice people, but we just didn't have that spark that we needed.

Today I'm a real baseball fan. When I played I didn't watch it that much but now, hell, when a ballgame comes on television my wife and me shut everything else off. I like to watch those Atlanta Braves, they're my favorites.

When I was coming up, I had a good friend in Apalachicola who had gone to the big leagues for just a few ballgames, named Ned Porter. I believe Ned Porter was one of the first ballplayers from Florida to make it to the big leagues. He had pitched for Bill Terry with the New York Giants. We hunted together and fished together. Ned was personnel director at the St. Joe paper company. When I was just a young, single wild kid he told me to come on and start working there so that when I got through playing baseball I would have a job for the rest of my life. So, I went to work there in

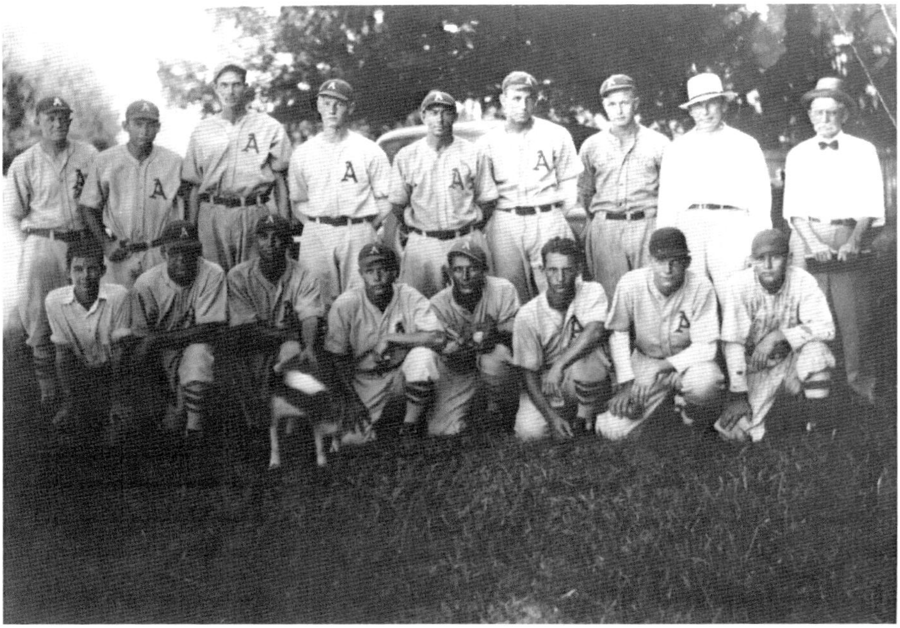

Apalachicola baseball team, ca. 1930s. Ned Porter is in the rear row, first from left. *Courtesy Florida State Archives.*

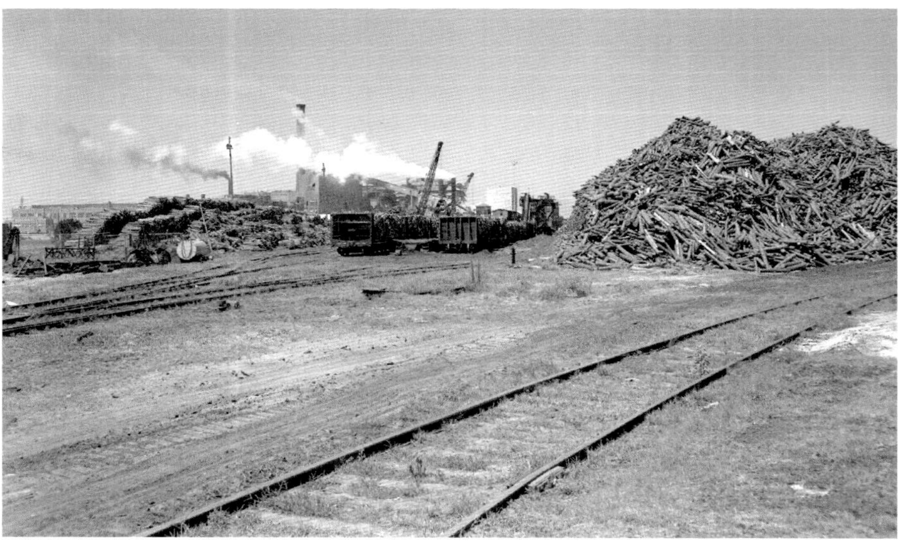

St. Joe paper mill. *Courtesy Florida State Archives.*

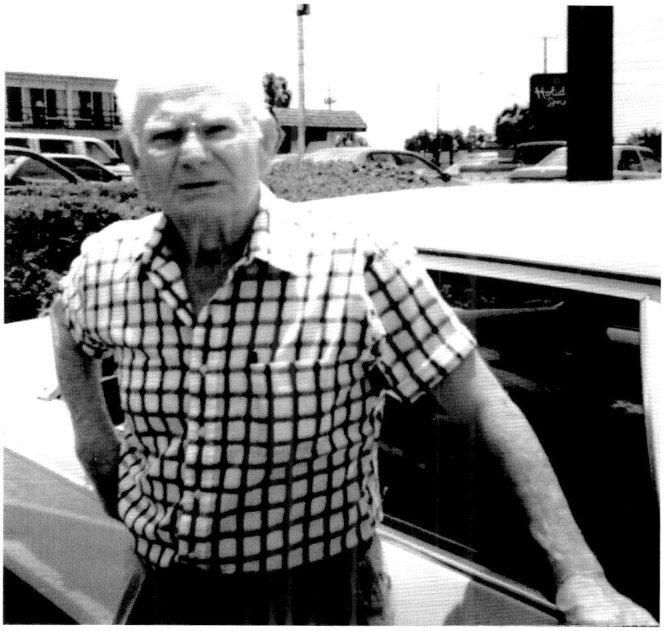

Jimmy Bloodworth, Tallahassee, Florida, 1993. *Photo by author.*

1939 and I worked every winter, except for when I was in the service. When it came time to retire I came home and went to work at the mill and just didn't go back to baseball. That's the way it was. The transition was real easy for me because I already knew all the fellows at the mill. We had a good time and I enjoyed working with them, we were all friends. If anyone got in bad shape financially we would take up a collection and pay him out of debt.

You know that I am in the Hall of Fame don't you? In 1946 Bob Feller broke the all-time strikeout record for one season. It was 348 men he struck out, and I know it was 348 because I was number 348. So they took the ball he struck me out with and put on the ball, "With this ball, in 1946, Bob Feller struck out Jimmy Bloodworth for the record 348th strike-out in a single season." It's at Cooperstown on display; you can see it.

Frank "Red" Barrett

St. Leo College
Athletic Hall of Fame
Elected April, 1987
Prep School 1928–32
All-Time Outstanding Athlete
16 Letter Winner
All-State Catholic Basketball Team
Major League Baseball

—Inscription from Red Barrett's Hall of Fame plaque
enshrined at Saint Leo College, Florida

Frank "Red" Barrett, the all-time outstanding prep athlete in the history of St. Leo College, made his Major League debut in 1939 with the St. Louis Cardinals. The long, lean Barrett was a crafty hurler, enjoying stops in Boston with the Red Sox and Braves, and at Pittsburgh. He also pitched for Hall of Fame manager Al Lopez while with the Indianapolis Indians of the American Association. His best season came in 1945 with the Boston Red Sox when he compiled a 2.62 ERA in eighty-six innings of relief.

I was born in Fort Lauderdale, Florida, in 1913, on the southwest corner of Second and Seventh Avenues. We lived in a home built by my daddy. Fort Lauderdale wasn't too large a community then. My daddy and a fellow out of Miami by the name of Gilfoil came down with the Flagler railroad. They were both bridge builders who were connected with the Flagler system. The first time they came to Fort Lauderdale was, I think, way back in 1895. They were building

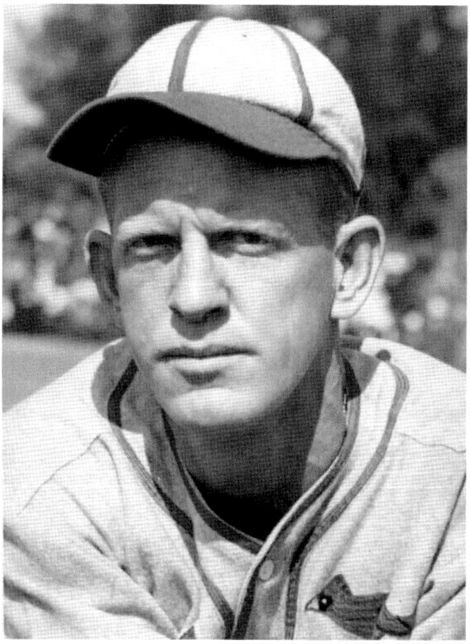

Rookie hurler Francis 'Red' Barrett with the St. Louis Cardinals, 1940. *Courtesy National Baseball Library, Cooperstown, New York.*

the Florida East Coast Railroad at that time. Although I don't believe that the two of them followed the line all the way to Key West.

I spent most of my youth as a kid in and around Fort Lauderdale. I went to St. Anthony's Catholic School there in Fort Lauderdale. I used to be around the ballpark and all but I never played in any games. The first baseball game I can recall attending in Fort Lauderdale was played about one block west of U.S. 1 and Second Street, right where the old "Flying L," Fort Lauderdale High School, used to be, about one block west of where U.S. 1 now goes under the river. In case you didn't know it, the "Flying L" was the high school logo. I imagine that was around 1920 or just prior to that.

I began attending St. Leo preparatory school around 1928, just before my freshman year in high school. St. Leo is now a college with a fine baseball program. It became a college in 1965 or 1966. They started with a two-year program but have since advanced to the regular four-year curriculum. Back when I attended it was a college preparatory school. I started playing baseball during my freshman year at St. Leo. I had never played the game before that. We lived about two and a half to three miles outside of Fort Lauderdale, in the country, and we had to ride the bus to school. If we missed the bus, why then we had all that way to walk home. That area is all developed now but at that time there was probably only about three houses in the whole area. Our place was just about a mile north of where the airport is at this time. Also near the airport back then was a nine-hole golf course and we used to earn a little money there, maybe fifty cents or so a round, working as caddies. Well, Mom had some milk cows too; a little dairy like, and we had our chores at home. There just wasn't very much time to be playing baseball.

Well, to continue my education my parents sent me off to St. Leo, it was a room and boarding school. I attended as a regular scholar and not on an athletic scholarship or anything like that. My folks sent me there from Fort Lauderdale. I think a good Catholic education was foremost in my parents' minds and that is why they sent me there. They wanted to give me the best start that they could. They weren't real wealthy people but they thought they would give their children an education. My two brothers went to a Catholic boys' school just north of St. Augustine and my two sisters went to the Catholic girls' school in St. Augustine. Everything turned out fairly well. They all ended up doing well in life, although I'm the only one of the Barrett clan left.

One day after I arrived at St. Leo, the class began playing baseball as part of their little intramural games. This particular day they happened to run out of pitchers—this one boy had been getting hit real hard—and the coach asked if anyone wanted to try pitching and I said that I would. So I went out there and started throwing and got them out pretty good. Well, that was the beginning of it for me, right there.

After that I began pitching for the school team and had some very good years. I earned sixteen letters in all during high school in baseball, basketball and track. In basketball I made Catholic all-state and used to travel on the road to play tournaments in places like St. Augustine and so forth. In track I was the high-point man at the state track-and-field meet four straight years and made Catholic all-state there as well. One year I had more points by myself than the entire team that finished second. I ran the hurdles, did the high jump and threw the discus and javelin. The Catholic state track-and-field meet was held in Jacksonville and was sponsored at the time by the Knights of Columbus. I also traveled to South Carolina once to participate in the Catholic southeastern championships. I was the only boy from Florida at the entire meet. We were just a bunch of kids having a good time and we did well.

About that time, I began pitching for the little town of San Antonio, which is about a mile away from the school. This wasn't the minor leagues, it was just town team baseball. They usually had ballgames on Sunday and Thursday afternoons and all the stores would close so everyone could watch. We played against teams from Dade City, Zephyrhills, Brooksville, Withlacoochee, Bushnell, the Tampa Union Painters, and Plant City—just town teams.

After watching me play a number of times, a fellow in Dade City named John Cain, who was originally from St. Louis and knew some folks up there, wrote to the St. Louis Browns on my behalf. I guess he liked my pitching. Not long after that I got a letter from Rogers Hornsby, the manager of the Browns, which I still have by the way, inviting me to come to spring training with them in the coming season, 1934. For some reason I didn't do it. I finally went to spring training the following year, 1935, with the Rochester team, who was training in Bartow, and was signed there by the St. Louis Cardinals. The Cardinals sent me to Albany, Georgia, to their Class D club, for my first season of professional baseball.

There were several boys there who went on to have good careers in baseball. Sam Narron played for a few years in the Majors. Rex Bowen went on to work in the scouting division for the Cincinnati Reds for a number of years. At that time Branch Rickey and his son ran the Cardinals. Albany was one of their many farm clubs. I think they had about sixty or so farm clubs spread around the country.

The team was known as the Albany Travelers and I pitched for them in 1935. We had quite a good little ball club. We played against Thomasville [GA], Tallahassee, Americas [GA], Panama City—we all didn't make much money but we had a lot of fun. I was only making sixty-five dollars a month. And meal money was a buck a day. You were lucky if you could save enough money for the train ride back home at the end of the season. If not, you had to borrow it to pay the fare. We all survived though.

I played against Jimmy Bloodworth that season. Bloodworth was playing for Panama City. He went on from there and had a fine Major League career.

In 1936 I left Albany and went over to play for the Columbus Jets in Columbus, Georgia, where Eddie Dyer was the manager. While at Columbus, I hurt my shoulder. I was in the outfield catching fly balls one day and I stepped in a little hole and it threw me off balance and when I hit the ground I separated my shoulder somewhat. So I spent most of that season just going here, there and yonder. Like I said, Eddie Dyer was the manager, and Enos Slaughter was there too, we had quite a bunch of boys. Slaughter was a good ballplayer even then. He was always a lot of chatter and a lot of hustle, all the time on the go. We had about two or three boys from that ball club that wound up playing a lot higher class of baseball. Mercer Harris went and scouted for one of the clubs up there for a long time. Francis Healy, a catcher, had been with the Cardinals. The year they played Detroit in the World Series, I think he had caught a couple of dozen ballgames for them. The Triplett boys were in Columbus. Coaker Triplett wound up playing for the Cardinals and Phillies for a number of years.

In 1937 and 1938 I was with Mobile, Alabama, in the Southeastern League and we won the pennant. There were teams in that league from Selma, Anniston [AL], Montgomery, Jackson [MS] and Meridian [MS]. After winning the pennant we went over to play Savannah from the South Atlantic League in the little Dixie Series and won. Jim Mooney, who later pitched for the Cardinals, went two games for us and I went two. We swept them four games straight. The next year we beat Macon in the same series.

In 1938 I played a bit as well for Rochester and after spring training we went north and opened up with a double-header in Baltimore. In the second game I pitched a three-hitter and the same fellow got all three hits and all three hits were home runs and I got beat 3–0. It was a big outfielder by the name of George Puccinelli. He was the one that got all the hits and runs. It was a little bandbox park in Baltimore and the outfield was real short. That was quite a deal there.

In 1939 I was with Houston in the Texas League and at the end of the season I went up and joined the Cardinals. We weren't with the team for very long. I think Harry Brecheen, Murry Dickson and Johnny Hopp, a first baseman, all went up with me at the same time. We were only with St. Louis for the last month of the season. We mixed in with the veterans pretty well but they had their own little cliques. They had been together all year. Now remember, I knew Enos Slaughter from our days in Columbus, but this was three or four years later and he had made a bunch of new friends and spent the summer with them. That makes a whole lot of difference on a club.

In my only appearance with the Cardinals I went in during the ninth inning of the last game of the season against Chicago with the score tied and right off put a man on. Then the next batter comes up, I think it was Peanuts Lowrey, with two outs and I made a pitch to him and he hit this little routine fly to left field, which should have been the third out. Pepper Martin was playing left and I remember him charging hard on the ball. But then he ran right underneath it and he just kept running, into the clubhouse, as the ball fell behind him and the run scored. I imagine he was in a hurry to get out of there. We were kind of being pushed by a train schedule; we left out of town right after the game. We still had to change clothes and pack and get everything ready to go. I guess nobody felt that it mattered if we lost because the team was already locked in second place and it was a meaningless ballgame in the standings. Personally, I felt let down that Martin could do something like that. That was my loss there for the season and that is the story behind my 1939 0–1 record. Sure, I had words with him after the game but there was nothing I could do, it was already finished. Martin was already an established Major League ballplayer and there was nothing I could tell him. I was just a kid coming up. I wasn't anybody and he was Pepper Martin.

In 1940 I was with Columbus, Ohio, the Columbus Redbirds, in the American Association. The American Association is Triple A, the top level of the minor leagues. I was with the Redbirds in 1940, 1941, 1942 and 1943. Then in about the middle of the season, 1944, I was sold to the Boston Red Sox and they called me up.

Columbus played in a league with Louisville, Indianapolis, Toledo, St. Paul, Minneapolis and Kansas City. There were some good players in that league. That was right next to the big leagues. Whitey Platt, another guy who made it to the Majors from Florida, was in that league with Toledo, the Browns' top farm team. Zach Taylor, another Florida guy, was the manager of Toledo then and went on to manage the St. Louis Browns. There was all kind of players there with the different teams that went on and starred in the Major Leagues. Duke Snider played with St. Paul—just a whole bunch of them. We all played together in the minors before all these future stars went up to the Major Leagues.

If we weren't teammates, we were enemies, but we all enjoyed playing against each other regardless. Preacher Roe and I roomed together in Columbus for several years. Preacher, who later pitched for the Dodgers, was a good pitcher, he could throw it. He was from down in Arkansas. He, his wife and little Preach, they went back to Arkansas after his playing days were over and he went into the grocery business, as I understand it.

All those boys that went up and made the National and American League clubs during those years came out of the American Association and the International League. I played either with or against most all of them. At Columbus, we won the American Association playoffs three straight years. Each time we played the winner of the International League in the Little World Series and won all three series. We beat Syracuse twice I think it was and they had both that double no-hitter that lives down in Tampa, Johnny Vander Meer, and Ewell Blackwell. Then the third year, we played Montreal and we beat them. We had a boy named Johnny Grasecci and he was quite a pitcher. He went into the service though and while in the service he messed up a knee. When he came back he could still throw hard but this is kind of a cruel game and he couldn't get around well so they went to bunting him. They would put down a bunt and he just couldn't get over to field the ball.

Kansas City was in our league and they were the Yankees' top farm club. Rizzuto and Priddy, that double-play combination, they were there. Hank Bauer, all that crew was there and we played against them. I pitched against some of the best players of the next era. Joe Garagiola was my catcher for a number of years at Columbus; he was a real nice fellow and he would remember me today if you asked him.

I stayed with Columbus right through most of the war years. Then the Red Sox, who had lost a majority of their team to the service, began looking for some pitching. I was doing quite well along about that time in Triple-A ball, so a deal was made and Boston purchased my contract and I went up and joined them. I stayed with Boston in 1944 and 1945 before being sent to the Boston Braves for the 1946 season. I had some pretty fair numbers with the Red Sox as a relief pitcher. In 1944 I led the team with eight saves. I also picked up eight wins, the most ever for me and had a 3.69 ERA over ninety innings pitched. The next season, 1945, my ERA dropped to 2.62 over eighty-six innings pitched.

Joe Cronin was the manager of the Red Sox, a real nice person. He played some shortstop, he and a boy they had named Eddie Lake. They had Jim Tabor and Bob Johnson, Tabor at third base and Johnson in the outfield. Dolph Camilli came and joined the club in 1945. Dave Feriss was a young pitcher on that team. I remember Feriss was from Shaw, Mississippi. He came up and joined us and had a good sinkerball. He kept the ball down and that was his main pitch and it was a real good one. His control was good and with that sinker he got a lot of ground-ball outs. He was a winner. Ferris won over twenty games a couple of times. Dave was an awful nice young man. I don't know what happened but he was out of the game fairly quick for someone with his early success.

I'll tell you this, pitching in Fenway Park, for a right-hander, was tough. You were always trying to keep the ball away from them right-handed hitters. You could go ahead and pitch normal to left-handers, but right-handed hitters you had to try and keep the ball away on account of the short porch in left field. As a right-hander I was usually brought in to face right-handed hitters and I was supposed to keep the ball away; that was the intention. But sometimes you slipped up and made mistakes. Hopefully, you didn't make too many mistakes because that is what Major League batters hit, mistakes.

You didn't pitch in relief as much during my day as they do now. I was watching a ballgame where the pitcher, Tom Glavine, was going along just beautiful into the seventh inning, leading 6–0, and they took him out. Why? It didn't make sense! Then comes the eighth inning and they bring in another pitcher and he gets through all right. Well, of course they take him out and in the ninth they bring in another pitcher and before he could do anything they had four runs against him. Now it's 6 to 4 and they have men on base with some power hitters coming to the plate. In our day when you went out there to play, hell, you pitched nine innings. I've seen guys pitch both ends of double-headers. You had to go in and earn your money then. How the hell are you going to have any record of complete games the way they do it now? Yet I guess on the other hand you can't blame the player because it's not his fault that he was taken out, it's the manager. Anyway, they brought a closer in and were damn lucky to get the win when they already had it won with Glavine in there.

The Braves weren't a bad club when I played for them in 1946. I think that we finished in third or fourth place. Billy Southworth was the manager. Alvin Dark was just coming up then, a good young ballplayer. Warren Spahn was getting started again after the war. Johnny Sain was the big man on the pitching staff then. Those two formed quite a pitching duo. Later on the cry went, "Spahn and Sain and pray for rain." By that time I was gone.

In 1947, 1948 and 1949 I was back in Triple-A ball playing for Indianapolis, the Pirates' top farm team. The last two years I played there for Al Lopez, from Tampa.

Lopez managed the club in 1948, 1949 and 1950. Tony Cuccinello was Lopez's assistant. We won the pennant the first year Lopez came in, 1948. Lopez even caught some games for us. He was an old catcher, you know, and would catch if we had some injuries. Lopez was certainly a nice man to play for and even then you could see that he was going to be a great manager.

I finished up my playing days back in the big leagues briefly with Pittsburgh in 1950. The Pirates were not a good team but they had some young talent, guys like Ralph Kiner. I only pitched in a couple of ballgames for them and after that it was over. I went into managing for the next few years but decided to give it up and I came home for good.

These days I just roam around and get in everybody's way, agitate everybody I can. Even though we have the boatyard next door and the telephone company with their tower right across the street we are still happy living here. We bought this place in 1948 and it's handy to everything. We've got a lot of memories, raised a family here, and when all the kids want to go somewhere everything is within walking distance. So

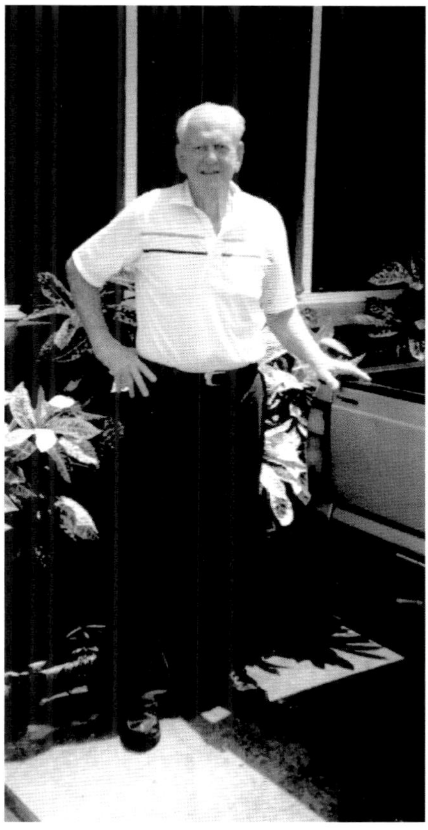

Red Barrett at home in Leesburg, Florida, 1993. *Photo by author.*

we are not too anxious to be packing up and moving out. We first came to Leesburg one year during spring training and decided that we liked the place. We came back whenever we could and eventually decided that this is where we would live. So during the off-season, in 1946, we moved down and I went to work. Initially I worked at packing citrus; this was a big citrus area back then. Then my wife Helen and I opened up "Red Barrett's Drive-In Barbecue Restaurant" in 1953 and we ran it for fourteen years. It was a place where the kids and all could go and we enjoyed it. Then I worked for a while with a filling station and after that retirement and social security.

Looking back on my career I can say that I enjoyed it all. I played hard and got out of it what I could. Though, there wasn't much money to be made. The most that I ever made in one season was $8,500, with the Boston Braves. I imagine that if I were playing today I could be making some pretty good dough.

Nowadays it seems that most young boys coming up are trying their hand at college ball first before going professional. If there is one thing I could say now, it would be to go and get your education. Anymore, most of your good players are coming out of the college ranks anyway. Programs like Florida State are sending them up there every year. Bob Tewksbury from St. Leo did all right with the Cardinals. Yeah, I would say to get your education first.

I still follow the St. Leo program pretty regular. I go down there to watch them play and get to see all the old-timers from my day, although there are not too many more of them around. Every year they have a banquet for the new inductees to the school's Hall of Fame, of which I am a member, and I go and hope to continue. In 1987 I was inducted into the Hall of Fame as St. Leo's greatest prep athlete. It was a great honor for my family and me. Out of all that crew of disciplinarians and priests from the time when I was there, only one is left, Father Marion Bowman. He went on later and was chosen abbot, although he is now retired. He is still over there though, and going along pretty good too. Father Bowman is always happy to see us when we go down. We all get together and have quite a time of it, mainly enjoying each other's company.

Andy Hansen

> They've [owners] treated ballplayers like property all along. If they got mad at you they sent you back to the minors. They could end your career very easily. I wasn't ready to quit when I did. After the way they treated me though, my wife said, "Lets go home, we'll eat beans." That is what we did.
>
> —Andy Hansen

Known primarily as a relief pitcher, Andy Hansen, who debuted with the New York Giants at nineteen years old, suffered the ill fortune of being traded away from the Giants to the Philadelphia Phillies during the winter of 1950. Hansen arrived in Philadelphia too late to be a "Whiz Kid," and left New York City before Bobby Thomson's homer off Ralph Branca sealed the 1951 National League pennant race for the Giants. Consequently, Hansen missed a pennant coming and going.

I think there were only about three thousand people living in Lake Worth, Florida, when I was growing up, maybe not that many. There were a lot of dirt streets and stuff like that. Nothing at all like Palm Beach County is today. It has really grown up around here since then.

As a child I only lived about a block and a half from the ball field. I used to go there, especially during the summer time, around eight o'clock in the morning, and I played ball until my mother called me around six o'clock at night to go home. I was at the ballpark all of the time. When I was about twelve or thirteen years old, I used to shag balls in the outfield for Eddie Miller and Mayo Smith as they practiced before going to spring training. Eddie Miller played shortstop for the Cincinnati Reds and Mayo Smith was with the Athletics. Neither of the two was from Palm Beach County

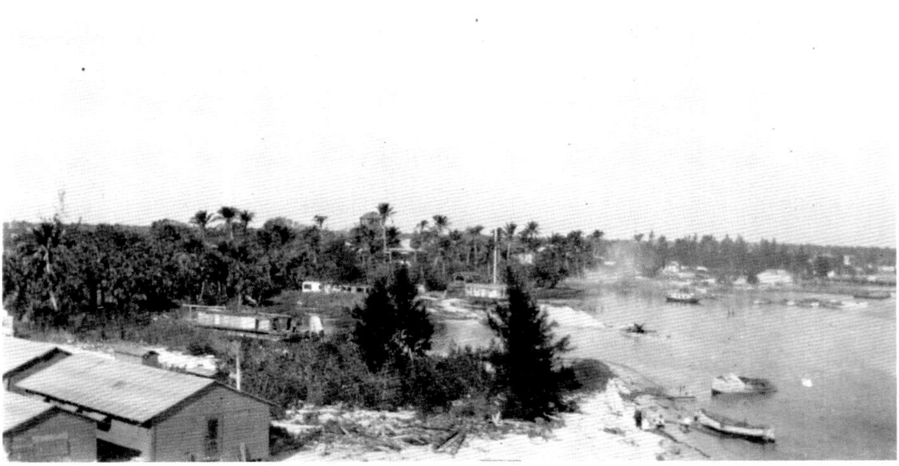

Lake Worth, Florida, 1930s. *Courtesy Florida State Archives.*

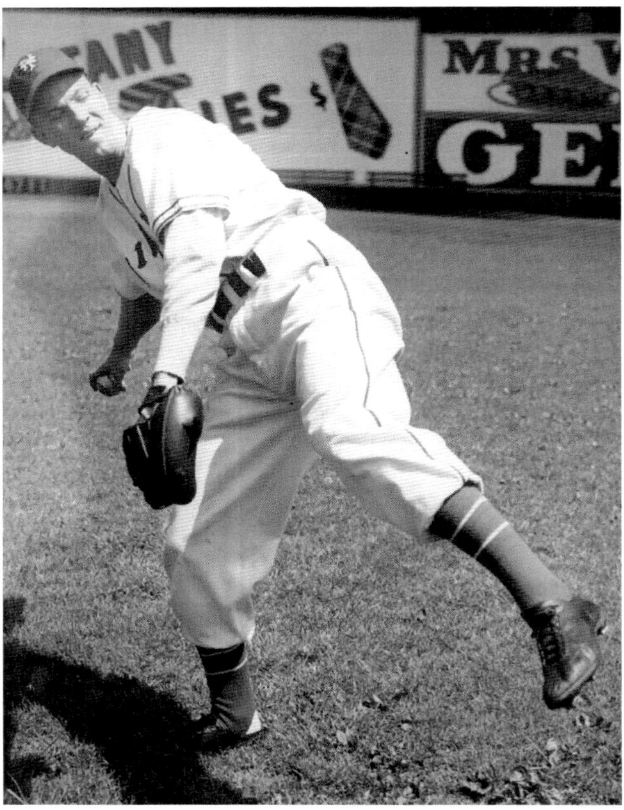

Andy Hansen, New York Giants. *Courtesy National Baseball Library, Cooperstown, New York.*

but they were living here then. Miller was still living over on the lake the last time I heard. Anyway, after I got to the Major Leagues I was thrilled to pitch against Miller after all of the time I had spent shagging flies for him as a kid.

Playing youth baseball then wasn't like it is today. They had some little clubs to play with but nothing near as organized as what they have now. The American Legion Hall might have a team or the Elks might have one. I remember that an ice cream parlor sponsored a team, stuff like that. They only had five or six all total. That was just for the young kids up to about twelve, thirteen or fourteen years old.

When I began in baseball I played second base mostly. Then they moved me over to third to take advantage of my good arm. One day, during my junior year in high school, they asked me if I wanted to try pitching. I gave it a shot and really enjoyed it. As I mentioned, I'd always had a good arm and that made me effective. I was a pitcher from then on. I attended Lake Worth High School, where I played just about every sport. Even though I had college scholarship offers to play football at a number of schools, including Georgia Tech, I chose to go with baseball. I think it was three days after I finished high school that I went to Bristol, Virginia, in the Appalachian League and began playing professional baseball.

It was 1943 when a New York Giant scout named George Mack signed me to a contract. We were playing in a high school baseball tournament up in Jacksonville and I pitched two games, winning both of them. After we returned home from the tournament, Buddy Goodell, the baseball coach at Lake Worth High, called me and said that he wanted to see me. So, Buddy Goodell and George Mack came over to the house and talked to my dad and me. We talked for quite a while and of course I was interested in playing baseball. So, we agreed to some things and they finally signed me to a contract to play for Bristol, Virginia, in the Appalachian League.

I didn't get a signing bonus or anything like that. In fact, the contract only read seventy-five dollars a month. On that kind of money you couldn't even afford to get home if you had to. Since the season had already started, the team didn't give me transportation money to get there either. So my mother and dad had to pay for it. I did get lucky though because when I got there I found this boarding house that only charged nine dollars a week for room and board. It was pretty cheap and we ate real well. My mother and dad also sent me a little money every once in a while; otherwise I couldn't have gotten by. They tried to help me all they could.

You might think that my parents would have favored my taking a college scholarship over signing to play pro baseball. That wasn't the case though. They figured that since it was what I wanted to do, I should go ahead and do it and that was pretty much it. Don't get me wrong, I would have liked going to college but I enjoyed baseball, so that's what I chose to do.

There were some fairly good players on the Bristol team. We had a good ball club. If I'm not mistaken, I think that we won our league by twenty-two games or something like that. The Appalachian League had teams in Bristol, Virginia, and Kingsport, Erwin and Johnson City, Tennessee. That is all the teams there was at that time. Since the towns weren't that far apart, we traveled to the games by car. It wasn't that bad because I think the farthest one might have been sixty or seventy miles away. The borderline of Virginia and Tennessee went right down the middle of Bristol. On Sundays, you could go to a movie on one side of the street but not on the other. The same thing with getting a drink; of course I didn't drink back then. Hardly anybody at that level drank back then.

I think that four or five players off that Class D club eventually went to the Majors. Bobby Cain, who pitched and played first base for us, went to the White Sox. A couple of others went into the service so I don't know what ever happened to them.

I left Bristol the following season and went to the Giants' International League club in Jersey City, New Jersey. I was there until late June 1944, when the New York Giants called me up. Looking back, I guess you could say that I went through the Giants' system pretty quick. At Bristol I went 13–3 and I think my record was 8–4 or something close to that at Jersey City. I also had good control and I guess that is what they needed, somebody with good control. The Giants called me up and Cliff Melton, who had been with the Giants for some time, went to Jersey City. Melton had won twenty games his first year in the Majors but never got back to it.

Gabby Hartnett had been my manager at Jersey City. Having a great old catcher like that as manager was certainly a help. Hartnett was a wonderful fellow and he could teach you quite a bit about pitching. He was just one of a number of big-name ballplayers that I either played for, with or against during my career. Whitey Lockman was a teammate at Jersey City. We were both only about nineteen years old at the time. Lockman followed me to the Majors the next season. We are still very good friends. Whitey is with the Florida Marlins organization in some capacity or other.

As I mentioned, I arrived in New York in late June 1944, and the Giants were right in the middle of a series with the Brooklyn Dodgers. The Giants and Dodgers rivalry was about as big as they got back then. Anyway, here I am a nineteen-year-old pitcher fresh from the minors and I go into a jam-packed Polo Grounds to play before fifty-five thousand people. I tell you there were more people in that stadium than probably lived in Palm Beach County at the time. It was really a thrilling thing to see—all of those people there at one time to watch a ballgame.

Mel Ott was the player-manager of the Giants when I arrived. He was just amazing. Even at that point in his career he was still playing quite a bit. Ott was very popular in New York, too, because he had been with the Giants since he was

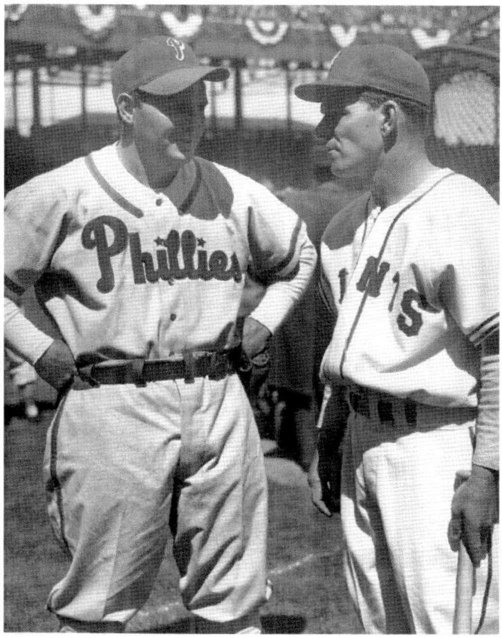

Mel Ott (right) and Ben Chapman, 1945. *Courtesy National Baseball Library, Cooperstown, New York.*

seventeen years old or something close. He was just a kid when he came up to play for John McGraw. But Ott was sort of a nervous fellow. He could get on edge pretty quick once the game started. We had our differences a few times. Once around 1947 or 1948, before he retired, he got on me hard because Jackie Robinson stole home while I was pitching. Of course, we were facing Brooklyn and Sid Gordon was playing third base and Walker Cooper was catching with Robinson on third. They had runners on second and third. When Jackie Robinson tried to steal home, Cooper, instead of trying to tag the runner, threw to third base. Well, Gordon wasn't covering the bag and the ball went sailing into left field allowing both runs to score. Somehow I got blamed for the whole doggone thing. I don't know, maybe Ott didn't think I held Robinson close enough to the bag?

Generally though, Mel Ott was real nice to me. He helped me out a lot. He had an assistant coach who was real good too. Oh, I can't remember his name. Back then we didn't have a true pitching coach like they have today. Now they usually have a pitching coach, a coach for catchers and everything else. Ott's assistant was just a regular coach who helped all over. The coaches really couldn't show a pitcher that much stuff back then. Either you knew how to pitch or you didn't, and if you didn't then you were gone. You usually tried to pick as much up off the veterans as you could. They were the ones who had been around and might be able to show you something useful.

The Giants were going through some down years when I joined them. They had a lot of older veteran players. Like I said, I was only nineteen years old when I got there and I think the average for everybody else was between twenty-eight and thirty. I had always been a starting pitcher but after arriving in New York they wanted me to go into the bullpen and pitch relief, because of my control. I liked to start ballgames but after going to the Majors it was mostly relief.

I think one year they let me start three straight games and I won all three. That was because Bill Voiselle, who had won about eight games to that point, had an argument with Mel Ott and was pulled from the rotation. We had been playing in St. Louis and the rule is that if you have two strikes and no balls on a batter then you waste the next pitch. You are not supposed to let the batter get a swing near it. Well anyhow, it was a real bad night, the wind started blowing like mad, it was thundering and lightning and we were ahead 2–0 with two outs in the fifth.

Bill Voiselle, who, like I said, was pitching, thought it was going to rain and he wanted to get the five innings in to record the win and we only needed the last out to do it. So, rather than waste one, he pitches to the guy and the batter pops it up. Well, normally it would have been a routine out but with the wind blowing fifty or sixty miles per hour and all, the second baseman couldn't get to it and the ball fell into right field allowing two runs to score. Then it got rained out. Well, Ott was mad as hell and fined Voiselle. If I'm not mistaken, Voiselle finished that season with only about 14 wins, and he had been 8–0 at one point.

In the later part of 1945 I went into the service and that kept me out of baseball for the rest of 1945 and all of 1946. The military had called me down to the Camp Blanding induction center three or four times, and finally on the last time they took me in. Initially I was sent to Fort McPherson and I sat there for three or four days. Finally, they posted a list that said I was going to Biloxi, Mississippi, to be stationed at Keesler Field in the air corps. I understand that they have gambling around Biloxi now. Well, they had gambling back then as well. You found slot machines everywhere you went. It's just come back around I guess.

I spent my entire military stay there in Biloxi. I was supposed to have been shipped out any number of times but I wasn't. You see, I played baseball for the Keesler Field team and every time I would get ready to go some place they would take my name off the list and keep me there. They wanted to keep me on their baseball team. We usually just played local teams or other military posts nearby. Sometimes we'd fly around to other bases to play. I had it real good at Keesler. The manager of our team was the head of the flight line and the coach was the head of the mess hall. So we ate good and flew wherever we wanted to go. It was easier to travel with the Keesler team than it had been in professional baseball. It wasn't bad living for the military either. Anytime we had an inspection or something like that I would go down to the flight line and take off flying with those guys. That kept me from having to go on maneuvers a number of times.

I really didn't play that much for them. I was only in the service a little over a year. I got out early, in 1946, because my dad got real sick. I came home to help take care of my dad. Since the war was over, they didn't seem to mind. Anyway, that is why I didn't play baseball in 1946.

I made it back to the Giants for the 1947 season and continued my role with the team as a relief pitcher. The Giants were doing about as they had before I left. But then, in the middle of the 1948 season, Mel Ott resigned and Leo Durocher came over from the Brooklyn Dodgers to take his place. We were in Pittsburgh when we began to hear rumors that Mel Ott was going to resign and Durocher was coming over. Of course we all thought that was a big joke. Nobody on or for the Giants liked anything about Leo Durocher or the Dodgers and vice versa. We didn't think that it could possibly happen. But then it did. He joined our team while we were on the road but once he got there he took charge. It was quite a shock when you think about it. Here was the hated manager of the hated rival and all of a sudden he is our guy. I'm sure that initially the fans had trouble with it too, but they came around.

Surprisingly enough, you couldn't help but like the guy. Durocher was always for his ball team, that's for sure. He was really a good manager. Durocher was for any

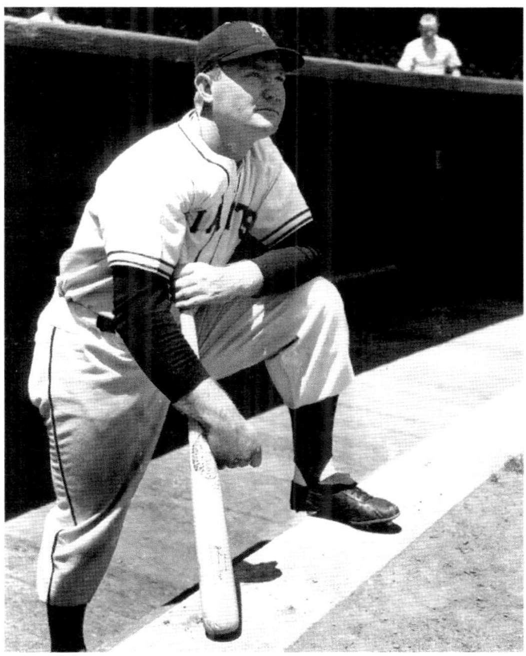

Johnny "Big Cat" Mize, New York Giants. *Courtesy National Baseball Library, Cooperstown, New York.*

way you could beat the other team. If you could win by doing this, then he did it. Everybody on the club came around to liking him in no time at all. He was always in the clubhouse talking with the guys. Mel Ott generally stayed by himself, kept his distance. Ott didn't mingle much with the ballplayers. But Durocher was a player's manager. Back then we didn't fly; we did all our travel by train. On trips the players would often play cards and Durocher would get right in there with them. He'd be right there agitating the players just like one of them. He was really good at keeping his players loose all of the time. A tight player can't win a ballgame.

Johnny Mize was a teammate of mine on the Giants. They called him "Big Cat." He could hit the ball. I think the year he hit fifty-one home runs, 1947, he must have hit about fifty of them six inches from the foul pole. Mize pulled a lot of them right down that foul line in right field and it was only 257.6 feet out there. I spent a lot of time with Johnny Mize. When we had time off, we used to drive over to Brooklyn in his big convertible Cadillac. One of our team sponsors, Hoffman Beverages I think it was, used to give us mixes and stuff for drinks and I used to give it all to Johnny Mize.

You got to that ballpark and the first thing you noticed were those short porches to either side. I mean they were right there on you. Everybody tried to pull the ball, so the only thing you could do was pitch him inside hoping they would foul it off. Then they might hit the next pitch 400-something feet to center field for an easy out. It was 480-something feet to center field when I played there and they took it out farther later on. Then back to the left-field side it was just 280 feet. So you couldn't pitch away from a batter on either side because they could go the other way for an easy homer. Pepper Martin hit a home run off me in the Polo Grounds and it went up and came down and hit right on the top of the right-field wall, 257.6 feet away, and bounced into the stands. Pepper Martin wasn't anything near a home-run hitter and this was at the end of his career. But he got one off me in the Polo Grounds.

Regardless of the standings, the Giants had some good players. It's just that back then, almost everybody had good players. They weren't all spread out like today. You could have a real good team and still finish fifth. An injury here or there is all it might take. I mentioned Johnny Mize. We had Walker Cooper behind the plate, Eddie Stanky at second; Alvin Dark at shortstop, Sid Gordon played third, Bill Rigney. A number of those guys went on to become managers. Bill Rigney, Alvin Dark, Whitey Lockman, Eddie Stanky all became managers. When you think about it, they must have learned a lot about managing from Leo Durocher for all of them to make it the way they did.

Sal Maglie, "the Barber" as he was called, played with us in New York. He had been with the team earlier but then went to Mexico to play in the Federal League. The way I understand it—I was in the service at the time it happened—they promised him all kind of money to play down there. The officials from that league came up to the clubhouse with $100 bills stuffed in their pockets and everything trying to get Maglie and some of the other guys to come down there with them. Maglie took the bait and was gone for about four years but then returned my last season with the Giants, 1950. From what I can remember, Maglie stayed by himself quite a bit. He was all baseball when he went out there to pitch, that is for sure. Maglie was a little bit like Durocher in that he later left the Giants and went to the Dodgers.

Larry Jansen, he taught you a lot, I liked Larry. In fact, Larry Jansen won twenty-one ballgames in 1947. We thought that he would be named rookie of the year, but Jackie Robinson won it. When you win twenty-one ballgames as a rookie and don't win rookie of the year, then that was a pretty doggone good year for rookies. Larry Jansen helped me out quite a bit with my pitching.

Of course I was young, but a lot of the older players took a liking to me in spite of it. Ernie Lombardi was always real nice to me. Lombardi, a Hall of Fame catcher like Hartnett, could teach you plenty. I sure liked old Ernie. In fact, one day after he'd retired, Lombardi was visiting New York and darned if he didn't come down to the bullpen and put his head over the fence and holler at me. You see what I mean though? Ernie was about thirty-five or thirty-six years old when I went up there. There were just a lot of older guys with the Giants when I came up.

Van Lingle Mungo and Johnny Allen were two veteran pitchers with the Giants then. Oh God, I thought Mungo would kill me one day. We were out in the bullpen just horsing around and I had a "Wilkie" pin or some kind of campaign button and I pinned it on him. When Mungo grabbed that thing to pull it off, it stuck him in his thumb. "You bush little bastard you," he said. Mungo chased me all over that field. It must have been quite a sight.

Johnny Allen was a competitor. I think 1944 was his final season in the Majors. Well one day he was pitching in Brooklyn and they used to have these buckets of water they sat by the dugout called "Florida water." This water had some kind of solution in it that was supposed to refresh you. They kept sponges in the water with ice and you would come in and wipe your arms and neck down to cool you off. Anyway, that day Johnny Allen was getting hit pretty hard and Mel Ott went out to talk to him. I guess Allen convinced Ott to let him stay in because he pitched to one more batter. Well, the next guy got a hit so Allen came out. Man, he came in mad and kicked both of them buckets of "Florida water" and I was sitting there and got soaked. It wasn't very refreshing either. I didn't say anything though.

Hank Thompson and Monte Irvin joined the club in 1949 as the first black players to play for the Giants. I didn't notice any problems from the other players over it. Of course, they came right in and won the National League pennant in 1951. Thompson was a lot smaller than Irvin was. He played third base. Irvin had been playing in the black leagues for years but he still had a lot of power. I remember facing him later on when I was with Philadelphia and I pitched him way outside. Well, he hit the thing and I thought it was a fly ball out to center. I turned around and all I could see was the number 1 on Richie Ashburn's back as he watched it go over the fence. Irvin hit that thing four hundred and something feet and yet I thought it was an easy damn out. Irvin had a lot of power.

Both Hank Thompson and Monte Irvin were real nice guys. Right after Jackie Robinson came into the league it seemed like the thing to do to help strengthen your team was to go out and sign a few black ballplayers. Well, the Giants weren't playing very well at the time so everybody wanted to work out with us. Sportswriters and what have you were always trying to bring someone in for a try out. Mel Ott would tell the press that we were going to work out so and so but then at the last minute he'd cancel it. There were probably ten or fifteen black players who wanted to try out with the team but were turned away like that. Maybe I shouldn't say anything, but that is what happened. I think the Giants were trying to keep them out as long as possible. But then the Dodgers and Cleveland, with Larry Doby, started to bring in the black players and soon everybody realized that if you were going to compete you had to bring them in as well. It wasn't until Durocher came over from Brooklyn that the Giants signed any black ballplayers.

Following the 1950 season, I was traded to the Phillies. If you check the records you will see that I missed a pennant going each way. The Philadelphia "Whiz Kids" won it in 1950 while I was still with the Giants and the Giants won it in 1951 after I had gone to Philadelphia. Remember, the Giants had that great stretch run to catch Brooklyn with the Bobby Thomson homer in 1951. I missed it! It was hard on me, sure, but to be honest, I was tickled to death at being traded to the Phillies. After all, they had just won the pennant with a young team and there was no reason to think they wouldn't win another.

Before the trade, I'd thought my career was over anyway. In 1950 I hurt my pitching elbow. I was going along fine one day until I threw a pitch that bounced about ten feet in front of home plate. I didn't feel any pain or nothing, so I threw another pitch and this one bounced fifteen feet in front of the plate. Well, Durocher came out wanting to know what was wrong and I told him I didn't know. I said that I'd heard something pop in my elbow but it didn't hurt or anything. So he took me out and I imagine that within about two hours my elbow got as big as a football and by that night it was all black and blue. To this day I don't know what happened. Well, I stayed in the clubhouse for about a week or so but when I tried to throw it wouldn't go ten feet. Well, the season wound down and over the winter the Giants traded me to Philadelphia.

I don't know if Philadelphia realized that I had arm trouble or not. I went to spring training over in Clearwater and I started throwing pretty good. The arm wasn't showing any signs of trouble; it just came around. Nobody did surgery back in those days. If your arm was gone, you were finished and that was it. Anyway, the Phillies broke camp and went back north and they sent me to Hollywood, Florida, to get a little more work in the warm weather. The Baltimore Orioles were the International League team affiliated with Philadelphia and they trained in Hollywood. My elbow popped on me once again while I was with the Orioles, but since it didn't bruise and everything seemed all right, the Phillies called me back up to the Majors.

Philadelphia had plenty of talent on their club. Robin Roberts was as good as anybody going at the time. Curt Simmons was pitching for them as well. He was a good ballplayer. Simmons could throw it ninety miles per hour or more. You know, Curt Simmons missed most of the 1955 season because he about cut his toe off with a lawnmower. He and Robin Roberts were very good friends. This one time Simmons was cutting along a bank or something and ran the lawnmower over his toe and practically cut it off. It cost him the rest of the season. You can't pitch with a bad toe.

Robin Roberts was in the middle of a great stretch when I got to Philadelphia. He had won twenty games in 1950 and went on to win more than that in each of the next five seasons. Roberts was really something to watch. He won twenty-eight games, I think it was, my first season with the team. I mean, watching him from the bullpen, you just couldn't believe what you were seeing. The way he pitched was deceiving because he threw with such an easy motion. He'd wind up and let it go and then, about half way to the plate, the pitch would jump up there and bite you. Roberts was confident enough to dare batters. He would throw you a fastball and if you had a good cut he'd think, great! and throw it harder next time. He was the kind of pitcher that was motivated by facing a tough hitter. Roberts never gave in to a batter and he would fight you right down the line. Robin Roberts was a wonderful guy and a Hall of Fame pitcher if there ever was one.

During my years on the Phillies, I roomed with Richie Ashburn. Ashburn could run as good as anyone playing baseball back then. He'd swing the bat and was already five steps down the baseline. Besides that great speed, he was a lifetime .300 hitter who led the league batting a couple of times. He played great in the outfield. Like I said earlier, talking about Monte Irvin, if the ball went near center field you assumed it was an out. Richie Ashburn was a great ballplayer.

Jimmy Bloodworth played a little second base for us. He had been in the American League for years and was winding down his career in Philadelphia. We didn't talk too much. I was in the bullpen mostly. He was a real friendly fellow though. Everybody liked him. But at the time, I didn't know he was from Florida.

Del Ennis had some good years for us. He hit the long ball and could play the outfield. Andy Seminick was the catcher. Dick Sisler was there. Eddie Sawyer was the manager. He was another good manager that I played for. However, Sawyer never said much. In fact, I can't recall ever having seen him in an argument with an umpire. That wasn't like Leo Durocher. Durocher was always out there arguing something.

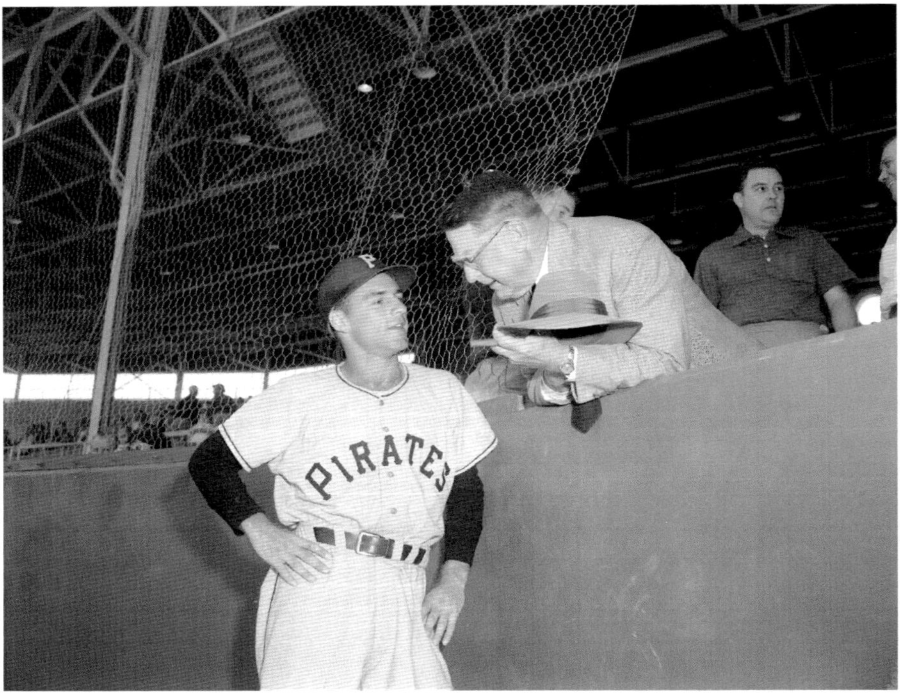

Branch Rickey (leaning over rail), as general manager with the Pittsburgh Pirates. *Courtesy Florida State Archives.*

Sawyer though, he sat back and took it easy. He did his managing from the bench and he was good at it.

I didn't pitch as much in 1953 as I had the previous two seasons, so in the off-season Philadelphia traded me to Pittsburgh. I think Murry Dickson came over to Philly in that deal. Anyway, I reported to spring training in Fort Pierce, Florida, ready to go. But after I got there I had quite an argument with Branch Rickey, the general manager, over how much I was going to be paid. Rickey wanted to cut me $750 on my salary and I wasn't making much anyway, but he said that if I made the club I would get the money back with a raise. So I figured well, OK. I'd planned on making the club. Then I got to thinking that I could get my ten years in if I stayed with the club at least thirty days to start the season or until cut-down time. Getting my ten years in was important to me.

Well, when the team got ready to leave Fort Pierce for somewhere in Alabama, working their way north, they told me that I was going to Hollywood, in the Pacific Coast League. I didn't want to go to California, so I tried to get in touch with Rickey but I couldn't get him anywhere. I'd thought they were going to keep me there at least the thirty days. So, I came back to Lake Worth, packed my family up and drove across the country to Hollywood, California.

After we got there and checked into a motel, I left my wife and two kids and reported to the team up in Oakland. I had to fly up there because that is where the team was playing. I stayed with them for a week and pitched all relief and was voted outstanding Hollywood player for that week. They gave me dinner at the Brown Derby and some other stuff for it. Well, I was still trying to get Branch Rickey on the phone and finally got him. I called him collect because I didn't have a phone, and he wouldn't accept the charges. So, I went and got a whole bunch of quarters and called him again. I told him that if I was going to stay with Hollywood I wanted the $750 back that he had promised, but he wouldn't do it. I said all right then, put me on the voluntary retired list, I'm going home.

You know, what I was asking for wasn't anything. Get my ten years in? Big deal! They give you a lifetime pass to all the games or something like that. And what was $750 to them? That is all it was. Well, I was only twenty-eight years old, but with a family I had to work, so we came on home. We had two flats along the way, the last around New Orleans and I ended up finishing the drive on bald tires and with about $5 in my pocket. We'd get on the road about two o'clock in the morning so it would be cooler on the tires and keep them from blowing out. Me, my wife and two kids on the road like that cross-country. Anyway, we made it.

After I returned to Lake Worth, I got another contract in the mail from Pittsburgh, this one calling for me to report to New Orleans in the Southern Association. Along with the contract they sent me my paycheck and I cashed it but still stayed home. Two weeks later they sent me another paycheck and I cashed it too. If they had given me that money earlier, I would have stayed in Hollywood. I got it anyhow! But because of it all, I retired when I was twenty-eight years old and I think I was pitching better then than at anytime in my career. I couldn't shop myself around either because I didn't know if Rickey would have given me my release.

I went to work for the postal department in Lake Worth. I had worked for them in the past. Every Christmas I'd come back and work for five or six weeks, or something like that. They wanted me back so I stayed there and worked with them for thirty-one years. I was in charge of all the windows, made all the deposits, had a lot of responsibility assigned to me. I enjoyed the job until I retired.

I never had much time to do any coaching or anything like that. Then my wife got cancer and passed away. I've remarried though. My present wife, Joy, is real nice. We used to go out together years ago. In fact, I had her come up to New York and visit me back in 1945.

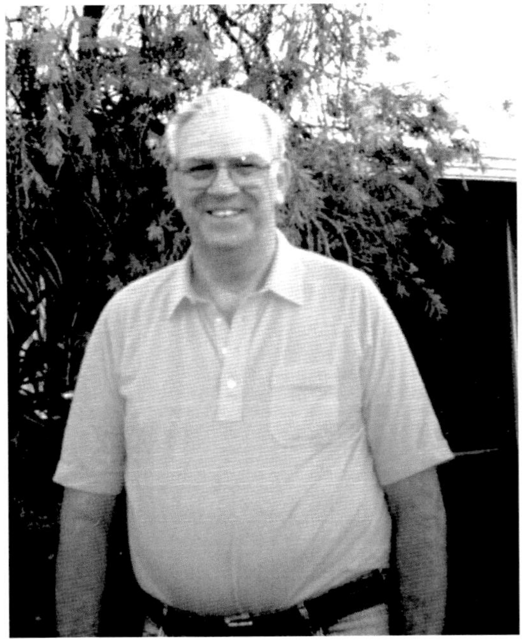

Andy Hansen at home in Atlantis, Florida, 1993. *Photo by author.*

My only regret in life is that I played baseball forty years too soon. I make more money in the baseball pension then I did when I played ball. It's hard to believe, but the first year I played in the Majors I made $3,300. I make $1,600 to $1,700 a month now off my pension. If I had played after 1957, which was possible because of my age, I'd probably make double what I make now. The owners were tight with the dollars back when I played. Johnny Mize hit fifty-one home runs in 1947 and had a hard time getting $30,000 the next season. I quit over $750!

They probably could have run four or five ball clubs with what one ballplayer earns today. But these owners don't know what they're doing. Some of them have all the dollars while others are struggling. The ones that have the money are going to get all of the good ballplayers. Teams fall apart because they can't afford to keep their players. I think that the owners are the ones who have brought all of the current labor problems on themselves. They've treated ballplayers like property all along. If they got mad at you they sent you back to the minors. They could end your career very easily. I wasn't ready to quit when I did. After the way they treated me though, my wife said, "Lets go home, we'll eat beans." That is what we did.

Elisha Matthew "Bitsy" Mott

> Around 1956, I had an opportunity to go and work for my brother-in-law who was the manager for a young singer. My brother-in-law was Colonel Tom Parker and of course the singer was Elvis Presley.
>
> —Bitsy Mott

Bitsy Mott broke into the Majors as a shortstop in 1945 at age twenty-six with the Philadelphia Phillies. For varied reasons, however, his career seemed destined for the minors, and, if not for World War II, he more than likely would have remained there. A gregarious and outspoken individual, Mott traveled the baseball circuit with stops in Tampa, where he was a local icon of sorts, Americas, Georgia, Utica, New York, and Miami. Following baseball, Mott went to work for his brother-in-law, "Colonel" Tom Parker, and a young singer from Memphis named Elvis Presley. The show, it seemed, was only beginning.

I was born down in Arcadia, Florida. I can remember as a child asking my mother, "Where in Arcadia was I born?" You see, Arcadia is prairie country. She would tell me, "On one of those prairies, I forget which one." Anyway, I had two brothers and three sisters; all were older than me. Of course, I have outlived all of them because I was the baby.

I began playing baseball as a kid in Bradenton, Florida, where my family was living at the time. I remember having a team when I was twelve years old that I liked to think of as a little "Gas House Gang." Those were the days of the great St. Louis Cardinals "Gas House Gang" teams and I used to skip school a little bit, every now and then, to go out and watch them in spring training. I would get to see Pepper Martin and that bunch, and they used to do all that fancy stuff with the baseball while they were warming up. It was great to see. They show a little bit of it on TV every once in awhile.

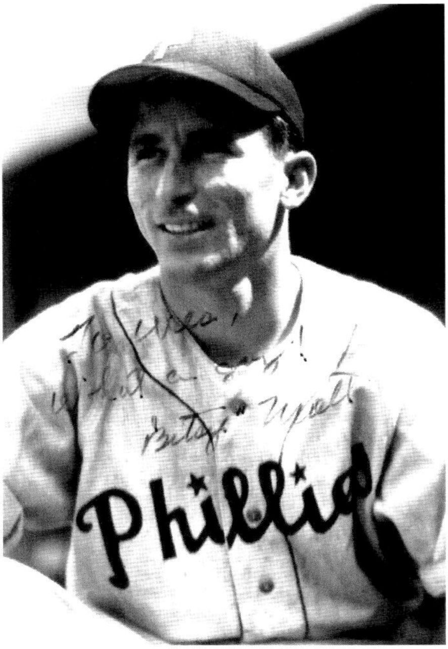

Bitsy Mott with the Philadelphia Phillies, 1945. *Courtesy Bitsy Mott.*

Anyway, like I said, I had my own baseball team when I was twelve years old. We used to meet out at Bradenton Field every Sunday morning at eight o'clock. Boy, my team was there too because they knew I was strict. I may have only been twelve but I could play the game and I took it serious. Since everyone else on my team was scared to get behind the plate, I had to catch. We played our games hard too; we wanted to win. We would generally play against other kids, pick-up teams that would come in. That team sure was a tough bunch.

By the time I was fourteen, I was playing for Bradenton in the Orange Belt League. This was an intercity league going on at that time. On account of my age, they would have to send somebody with me as an escort. Then of course, I went to Bradenton High School and played second base both my freshman and sophomore years. My team at Bradenton, the Gold Wave, won the district championship one year. We beat Hillsborough High School from Tampa. I made all-conference and all-state. After that, however, my father moved us to Sarasota and of course Bradenton didn't appreciate that a bit. They used to really try to get a hold of me in football. Anyway, once at Sarasota we would beat Bradenton and that would burn them up. I played baseball, basketball, football and tennis at Sarasota.

When we lived in Bradenton, my father had run a fish market. But when he moved us to Sarasota it was because he found work building a bridge that crossed over from

Sarasota to Bradenton. It was one of those concrete bridges and my father was both a blacksmith and an ironworker. He did a lot of iron working on that job. The bridge is still there.

From that point on I kept improving my game, getting a lot of notice, making the all-star teams and stuff like that, and that got the scouts to watching me. That was fine with me, too, because I already had my mind made up on professional baseball. So one day, this guy named Butch Henline, who had taken a liking to me, said that he was going to bring in a Brooklyn Dodger scout to watch me play. Henline was one of those catchers who could sit on his haunches while he threw to second. He had been a good player—played in the Majors with Philadelphia and Brooklyn—but he was an ornery old thing. Anyway, the Brooklyn scout came and he hit me ground balls until he could hardly stand up and I don't remember missing any of them. I was just eating those balls up. Of course, that is the reason I made the Majors later on—glove, speed and bunt. Well after the tryout, he signed me right up. Later on I found out that Henline got $500 bucks for it, I didn't get nothing.

After I signed with Brooklyn they sent me to Americus, Georgia, to play in the Georgia-Florida League. When I got there, I went out to the ballpark and there were five shortstops already there. I was the sixth! I wondered what the hell was going on. I had figured that it would be just me and maybe one or two others. Well, you know who ended up there. I ended up there because of one particular play that I could make that none of the rest could make. When I had first worked out for that Brooklyn scout, he had taught me this way of fielding the ball in the hole behind third. What I would do was slide into the ball while fielding it and then drop the ball from my glove into my throwing hand all in one motion. Then with my strong arm I would fire it over to first to get the out. It was really something to see and it was something that none of the others could do. In this fashion I could really go get them in the hole and that is the hardest thing for a shortstop to do.

Well I was the shortstop for Americus that season, 1939, and was having a good year with the club, although the team wasn't very good. Then late in the season, in a game against the Cordele Bees, I hurt my ankle pretty severe, a bad sprain, and it took forever to heal. My trademark had become the way I could slide after those grounders and now I couldn't do that. Well because of my slow recovery, Americus, late in 1940, sold me to Gainesville, in the Florida State League, but since I couldn't play, I left there and got a job with the Seaboard Coastline Railroad.

While with the railroad I played a little ball in the Inter-Social League in Tampa. It was an amateur league made up of guys playing for the various social clubs in and around Ybor City. Anyway, they had some good players, many of whom later played for the Tampa Smokers in the Florida International League. I played for Centro

Asturiano. The Cuban club was always tough; they had Charlie Cuellar pitching and Manuel Fernandez catching. Guess what? Here is a funny thing. Bad ankle and all nobody had caught me stealing all season long. Well, this one game I was playing against the Cuban club and when I tried to steal second Manuel threw me out, the only time I was caught all year.

Lou Piniella used to pitch in that league too. Not the Lou Piniella you see on TV today in the Majors, his dad. He was a nothing ball pitcher; he didn't have nothing on it; pretty good control but nothing else. I even pitched in that league. I had a 4–0 record with perfect control. I had a slider and I don't even know how I threw it. Well anyway, my ankle started getting better about midway through the second year and I started thinking about playing serious baseball again.

I stayed at the railroad for the rest of 1940 and all of 1941 and 1942. Then in 1943, I had a chance to get back into baseball with the Utica Blue Sox, a class Triple-A ball team. But when I went to explain to the railroad that I was leaving to play baseball they said that I couldn't go. They told me that with the war on, there was a job freeze in such positions and that I couldn't quit. Well damn it, I had a family to support and the railroad wasn't paying me anything so I asked if I could take a leave of absence and they granted it to me. They haven't heard from me since. Hello, railroad!

Well, I went on up to Utica and pretty much picked up where I had left off, playing real solid baseball. I had a good season for them in 1943 and had another good one in 1944 before I was called up to the Phillies. We had broken all the records for double-plays in that league. Of course, I had made the all-star team. I had the scouts watching me all year. So at the end of 1944, Fred Daniels, Vance Dinges and I went up to the Majors. Now you can check the official record and it won't show that I ever played in 1944 but it is wrong. I was called up at the end of the season and did get into a little action, just no at-bats.

When I arrived in Philadelphia at the end of the 1944 season, Connie Mack was still managing the Athletics. Mr. Mack thought enough of my ability that he made a statement to the *Philadelphia Enquirer* saying that I looked like one of the best shortstop prospects he'd ever seen come up to the Majors. He said that I compared favorably to Jack Barry, who was his shortstop in the famous "$100,000 Infield." Jack Barry was the shortstop alongside Stuffy McInnis, Eddie Collins and "Home run" Baker. Now personally, I think that was some statement.

Well, the next spring season we were playing an exhibition game against a naval base team in Rhode Island. Anyway, they had me on third base because they had just paid $20,000 for a shortstop out of the Pacific Coast League that was supposed to be pretty good. They put me on third base and oh man, I loved it. I love it! I eat it up! Man, that arm I had, I just put it on them. They put a couple of bunts down and I came in, grabbed them, zoom, over to first for the out. I played errorless ball—even got me a couple of hits. I have to admit I played a heck of a game. That was my mistake.

The commanding officer of the naval base comes over to me after the game and is walking me to the clubhouse when he asks if I had been in the service. I said, "No sir." He asks me if I was going in and I told him that after dodging them for three years I hoped not. He asks, "What do you mean dodging them?" I told him that I would get the application during baseball season but when I let them know that I was moving to Florida or back to Utica that would delay it. The delay usually lasted long enough for me to move again–one big continued delay. They never could catch up to me, but it wasn't on purpose or anything like that. I told the officer that I wasn't intentionally dodging the military but I was pursuing my life's ambition of playing Major League baseball.

Well, this officer tells me that if by chance I was inducted into the service that year, there would be a big sergeant, I forget his name, Polish, that would be waiting for me at the induction center and that I wouldn't miss him. The sergeant was about six foot five, 250 pounds. He said that they had the best club in the whole circuit now and that all they needed was a third baseman and that he hoped I was it. I just said, "Yes sir!" You know that twelve days into the season, I'm batting .305, playing third base like nobody had seen, and here comes those papers. That officer pulled some strings. So, I went to the induction center and here that big Polack was. I said, "I'm Bitsy Mott," and he says, "I know it." So he told me to follow him and you know all them long lines, I didn't have to get in and out of them, I went around every one of them.

I'd had migraine headaches since I was about eighteen years old. I had a thick pack of letters from doctors, headache doctors, doctors that twist you around, foot doctors, all kinds of doctors. None of these doctors could find the reason for my headaches. Well, at the end of the induction, after I had skipped all of the lines where they were giving physicals, they put a big old stamp on there, "Naval Service." In spite of those headaches it was all cut and dry. That officer wanted a third baseman and I was it.

Well, I went on out and participated. Ford Garrison, who had been with the Athletics, was in my platoon. Me and him went on out, although he was more conscientious than me. He also wasn't getting the migraine headaches that I was and still do. I went out there and of course we ate steaks and salads, we didn't have to eat that garbage those other guys ate. Well, one day I said to myself I'd never get out of there if I went on and played ball, so I guess I started goofing off. They finally sent me over to the hospital to try and find out how to get rid of my headaches. None of the doctors could find out what was causing them and of course that didn't surprise me because nobody else had ever figured it out.

Finally I get in the room in front of all those people you're supposed to see when you are getting out of the service. "So you played Major League baseball?" they asked. "Yes sir," I replied. "You mean that you can play Major League baseball and you can't serve in the armed services?" I told them that there was a lot of difference between playing for three hours on a ball diamond and being subjected to stress for twenty-four hours a day like you are in the service. I was serious about it too. I used to get up at night with headaches and just walk the floor. The sentries would come by and look at me and tell me to get to bed. I would tell them that I'd been to bed and couldn't sleep; I was trying to walk off my headache. Anyway, it was all very legitimate. Those headaches were giving me a fit. Although, looking back I realize that I probably could have made a little more effort at it.

Well, all this only took about six weeks. When I got back, the traveling secretary for the Phillies, a guy named Alexander, calls me in Tampa, Florida, and says that they want me back up in Philadelphia. I asked him if they had a house for my family to live in. He thought that I was kidding. He asks, "What do I have to do to get a big-league ballplayer today?" I told him to get a house for my family. A day or two later he called and told me that he had a house and that the travel tickets were on the way.

The team was playing in New York when I arrived and they told me that I was going right in. I hadn't been working out on the naval base because of the headaches. We were playing the Giants, Mel Ott managing them. There is a funny story about that too. We used to visit the city that the Giants were moving out of and I always used Mel Ott's locker. All that I had to do was erase out the dot on the nameplate to change M. Ott to M Ott. The clubhouse men loved it. Anyway, I got to the game late because my family was with me. The clubhouse was in center field and the dugouts were a long way off. I had to cross the field to get to them. Philadelphia had just finished taking infield and so the field was clear. You want to talk about being embarrassed? Here I am, little five-foot-eight guy, 150 pounds, running across the field in a Phillies uniform and I know that them thirty thousand people up there are saying look at this little joker here coming in late. I felt embarrassed. Anyway, I got right into the lineup and started playing.

You can believe that the pitchers were way ahead of me at that point in the season. That accounts for my little old batting average going down to .221 from the .300-plus that I was used to hitting. Of course they couldn't get me out when I bunted; I could lay that thing down. Well, for the rest of the season I played terrific defensive shortstop. Ben Chapman, the manager, used to call me in and tell me not to worry about 1946 because I was his shortstop. Most everyone was worried for their jobs in 1945 because it was becoming obvious that the players in the service could be returning by the next season. Chapman and I had never had an argument. He called me in about three times just to reassure me.

The team itself was not a good one. It had some good older players but they were on their way out. Jimmy Foxx was on that team and so was Vince DiMaggio. Mostly though, it was guys like me who didn't have long careers in the Majors: Coaker

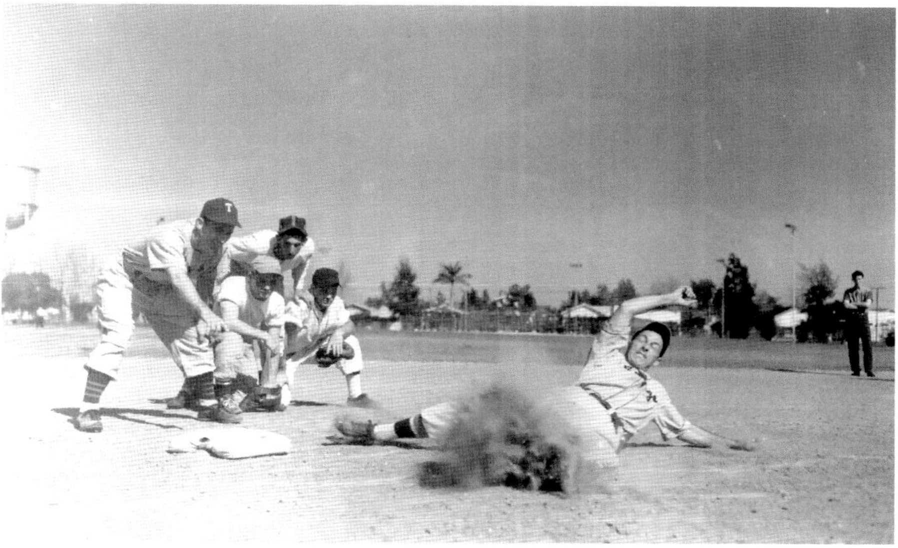

Bitsy Mott delivers slide technique instruction at the Tampa Baseball School. *Courtesy Florida State Archives.*

Triplett, Jimmy Wasdell, Fred Daniels, Vance Dinges and John Antonelli to name a few. We lost over a hundred games in 1945, but remember, I wasn't there for all of them. Believe it or not, I made the all-rookie team that season.

Well, 1946 gets here and we go to spring training in Miami Beach, Florida. Remember, I'm well known in Florida after having grown up there, playing in all those amateur leagues. Chapman wouldn't play me in exhibition games or nothing, just sat me on the bench. So here comes the big *Miami Herald*, they was all for me. They run a headline that reads "Is Chapman saving Mott for the all-star game?" I wish that I had cut it out; I don't have it anymore. Anyway, I'm getting disgusted about that time myself. I'd be so bored that during practice I would lay down in the outfield with my hat on my head. I was about as egotistical as Chapman and he was damn egotistical. One day I am sitting on the bench during an exhibition game while a guy named Stewart played shortstop. In the second or third inning, I forget, Chapman tells me to pinch-hit. Well I wasn't no pinch-hitter or long-ball hitter. The game is 1–0 in their favor, one out with a man on. I go up to bat and hit a double to the left-center-field fence. The hit scored a run that tied the game. There is still one out. The next batter hits a grounder to shortstop and I scored from second base! They threw the man out at first and I came home with a great slide and we won the game 2–1. No one could slide like me. Anyway, do you know that Chapman didn't play me again after that?

To this day I don't know what the reason was for Chapman putting me on the bench. It could have just been a clash of egos. I do know that their regular shortstop before the war was coming home from the service, but he wasn't there yet. But even so, he had never played for Chapman. Chapman took over from Freddie Fitzsimmons in 1945. Well, later on Chapman wished he'd kept me. The Phillies sent me back down to the Triple-A club at Utica, New York. Eddie Sawyer was the manager at Utica and he knew that I was disgusted. One day he came up to me and said that he had what I wanted. When I asked what it was he told me my release. I said great!

I went back down to Tampa, Florida, and began playing in the Florida International League with the Tampa Smokers. I made more money playing for Tampa than I'd been making in the Major Leagues. This was 1946 and you could make a lot of under-the-table money playing for Tampa. Financially, I came out a lot better but professionally it was a mistake to do it. I think back now and I am certain that just about any other Major League team would have given me a shot at shortstop but I was disgusted with it and went for the easy dollars. Remember, Philadelphia had given me my release. It is not as though I had just left the team and was still bound to them. Back then you were obligated to a club as long as they owned you. I could have gone anywhere and I went to Tampa.

I played for Tampa in 1946, 1947 and 1948. Because of all that under-the-table money that was coming in we were able to attract some real good ballplayers. We had a tremendous rivalry with the Havana Cubans. When Havana would come to town they would have to rope the field off to keep the fans from coming onto it. All those Cubans in Tampa would pack Plant Field for our games against Havana.

Late in the 1947 season Havana came into Tampa and Charlie Cuellar, who was pitching for us, threw a no-hitter against them and the place went wild. Those Tampa fans just loved it. But I'll tell you, there is a little controversy surrounding that no-hitter. Now I'm not saying this to down Charlie but he had friends on that club. Charlie was a local-born Cuban. He used to talk Spanish together with them and all that. He'd even played some ball with a few of their players. Well, the last batter up, I can't recall his name but a real good friend of Charlie's, just waved at the pitches for the final out. It was something that looked bad for both clubs really. I'm sure that it did for Charlie. It wasn't planned out in advance or anything like that but the guy did intentionally make the out. Now of course, eight and two-thirds worth of batters went down without a hit so it wasn't all bad. I'm just telling you what happened.

I used to room with Charlie Cuellar when we went on the road. His arm was so bad that I used to have to rub it down for him before every game he pitched. They used to call me "Mother Mott" because of the way I babied him. That was Charlie's problem when he went up to the Majors, they tried to use him in the bullpen and he couldn't take that. If he pitched one day he had to lay off for three or four days. But if you gave him his rest, Charlie could pitch. If he hit the spots with that exceptional curveball of his, he was a tough man to beat.

We had some quality pitching on that team. Besides Charlie Cuellar we had a one-eyed pitcher who came from Cuba named Rupert. Nobody would sign him because of his sight. This guy had a curveball like nobody's business. We also had Chet Covington with us. He had been on the Phillies for a time but I think he got into a fight with Andy Seminick, the Philadelphia catcher, and they shipped him for it. Covington had real good stuff; he could smoke it.

Tampa had some good hitters as well. Lamar Murphy played left field but didn't have much of an arm. I used to have to go way out into the grass to get the ball from him. He couldn't run or field much either but boy could he hit. Murphy had a big-league bat for sure. Benny Fernandez, our first baseman, was a real good low-ball hitter. You throw that ball down there low and he would hit it out of the park. He led the league in home runs one year. Manuel Fernandez, Benny's brother, was our catcher. He wasn't the hitter that Benny was but he could flat out catch. And we had fill-in guys like Joe Benedito. You can't discount the role on a team that a player like Joe has because they are important. That little Joe Benedito always kept me laughing. He was good to have on the club. If an infielder left for whatever reason, we would sign Joe to fill in for us at that position. He was a small guy but had a big personality.

Tony Cuccinello was Tampa's manager in 1947 and I loved it. He was the greatest guy to play for. Cuccinello was also a great manager. He could have been a manager all of his life but didn't want the responsibility. He stuck with Al Lopez and ended up having a good career with him as a coach. I'll tell you this, some people have said that Cuccinello stayed in the big leagues so long as a coach simply because he and Al were friends. That is a bunch of bull. I look at it the other way around. Al was such a success because he had Tony Cuccinello at his right hand. If you will look at the record you will find that Al never went anywhere without Tony. I admire Al Lopez, me and him are good friends, but Tony Cuccinello was something else. He was one of the best managers I ever played for.

In 1948, after Cuccinello left Tampa to join Al Lopez in Indianapolis, Joe Abreu came in to take his place. Joe was a good manager. He'd played a little with Cincinnati in the Majors. Joe and I used to run a baseball school in the off-season. It was real fun to teach at that level. I used to instruct bunting and sliding and all that. One of the things I remember most about the school was this advertisement we used. It said that we would "endeavor to place every student showing promise in professional baseball." Now that was a sales pitch! Can you imagine making that kind of statement today?

In 1949 I left Tampa and went to the Palatka Azaleas in the Florida State League to manage. Besides managing, I played second base and hit .305. In 1950 the owners sold me half interest in the club, but that was a mistake on my part. If you will check

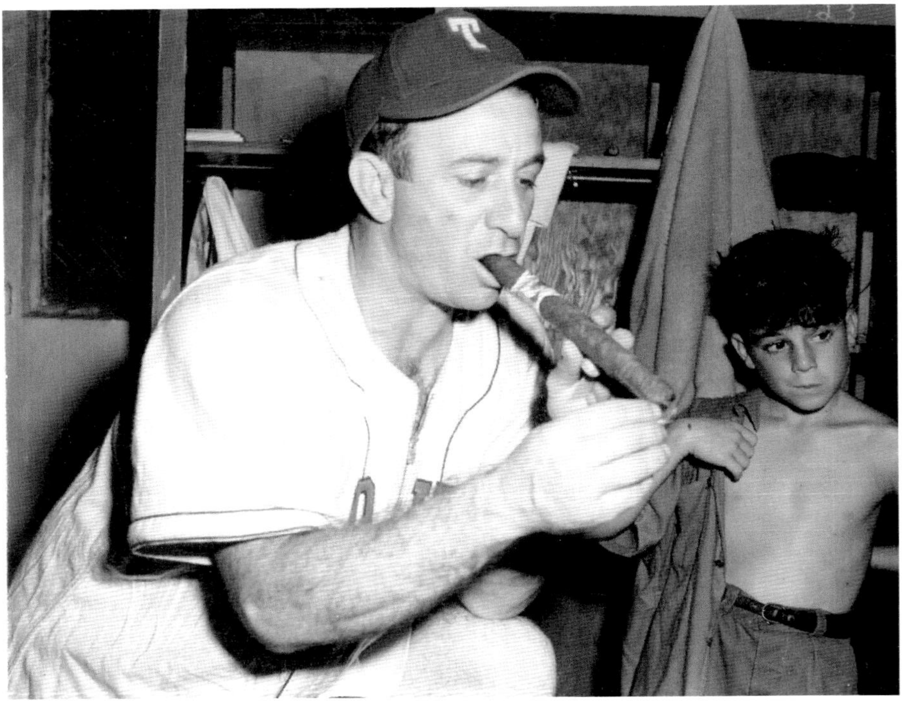

Tony Cuccinello, manager, Tampa Smokers, 1947. *Courtesy Florida State Archives.*

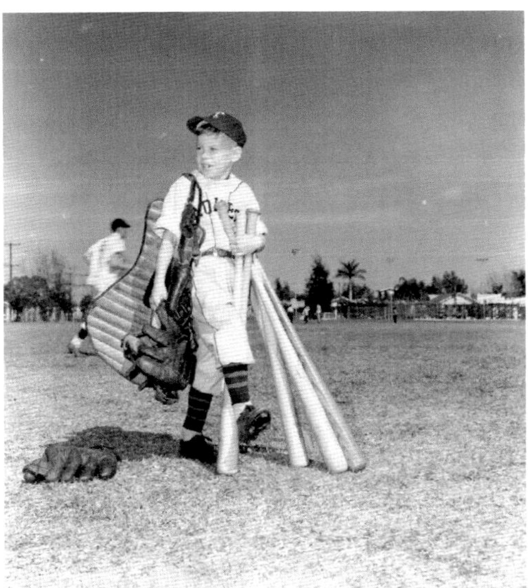

Jimmy "Smoker Jr." Mott, working hard at the Tampa Baseball School. *Courtesy Florida State Archives.*

the record books you will find out that 1950 was the lousiest year ever in baseball history for attendance. In 1949 the team had drawn fifty thousand people. I thought I had a good deal going but I was wrong. I lost my shirt on that one, ended up sacrificing my ball club to the city so they would make the salary payments. The uniforms, the bus, the whole deal went to the city. And then the city came to me and said the next sacrifice was going to be my salary. Well, I wasn't coming free to nobody so I left. I lost my home on that one as well.

After I left Palatka in 1950, I took off and started playing for West Palm Beach. Of course West Palm Beach played against the Tampa club and guess who had come down there to manage them? Ben Chapman! I don't know when he got there but it was somewhere between 1951 and 1953 because I retired from playing baseball in 1953 and I was with West Palm Beach at the time. Anyway, I came into Tampa to play against the Smokers and Rupert, that one-eyed Cuban curveball pitcher, was going for Tampa. Well anyway, that afternoon I went by a billiard room that I used to play a lot of pool in, a pool hall really, and the same old fans that were always in there saw me. Tampa was wide open on gambling then, people would bet on anything. They were heading to the ballgame where they would sit out behind right field and gamble. They would bet money on every pitch and every batter and everything. Anyway, I go by there and one of the boys, one of my fans, says, "Hey Bitsy, how about hitting me a home run tonight?" Well, I wasn't a home-run hitter but I told

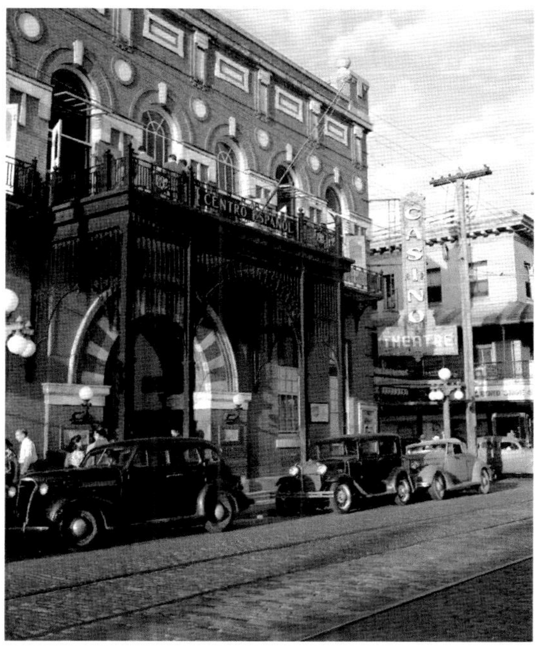

Centro Español Casino. *Courtesy Florida State Archives.*

him, "Guess what? I'll darn sure do it for you and I will call the shot so you better be watching." They all thought that I was kidding. So the game starts and about the fourth inning I come to the plate. First I take a pitch and then out of the clear blue sky I step from the batter's box and pull a Babe Ruth. This is the honest truth. I step out of the batter's box and look over at them fans and they hollered and screamed and I just pointed to the fence. Well, Rupert let go of the pitch and on cue, I hit that ball out of there. I guessed right on curveball and just hit it on the nail. Anyway, I hit the ball out and I'm rounding third base when Ben Chapman hollers, "You didn't hit like that for me," and I hollered back, "You didn't give me a damn chance!" Sometimes things have a way of coming around.

In 1953 I finished with West Palm Beach and that was the end of my baseball career. I left there and returned home to Tampa where I bought a tavern. I thought that it was a tavern but it was a bar if you want to know the truth about it. It was in the worst section of town that I could have bought in. It was on Fortieth Street, way over on the other side of Ybor City. I knew that it was a bad bar but I cleaned it up and tried to do something with it. I would stop a fight, walk the troublemaker outside to separate them and by the time I came back through the front door another fight would have started. How are you going to handle something like that? Anyway, I got out of it.

After I left the bar, around 1956, I had an opportunity to go and work for my brother-in-law who was the manager for a young singer. My brother-in-law was "Colonel" Tom Parker and of course the singer was Elvis Presley. The Colonel had married my older sister. He liked to call himself the dogcatcher while he lived in Tampa but he was actually in charge of the Humane Society. I'll tell you a story about that. Stores used to donate dog food to the Humane Society and sometimes he would take the dog food to another store and trade it in for real food that he would take home to eat.

Anyway, to start off, Colonel Parker said that he needed somebody responsible to haul Elvis' pictures and programs around to the concerts. They bought me a brand new 1956 Buick station wagon and we'd load that thing up and take off. When we got to the concerts I'd set up and just sell all that stuff. I always outsold everybody. Well, one day the Colonel comes to me looking for Elvis but I didn't know where he was. We were at an auditorium in Lincoln, Nebraska. So, he tells me to go and turn my books into Marie, my sister, and take off looking for him. I asked him where I should look and he said the movie theaters. Well, there weren't but two theaters in Lincoln at that time and I found him sitting in the first one watching a cowboy movie. He was down there in front eating popcorn with his cousin who used to travel with him. I sneaked in back of him and told him that he was due on stage. I said, "Elvis, you got eight thousand people down there hollering and screaming and we've got an Irish tenor coming back on stage for about his

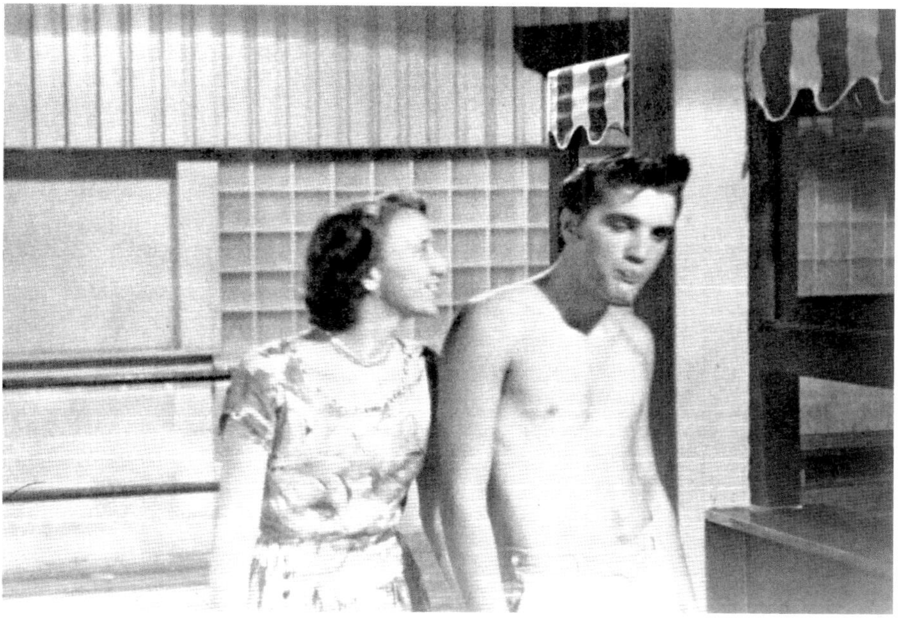

Elvis Presley in Jacksonville, ca. 1950s. *Courtesy Florida State Archives.*

fifth encore and they are about to throw him off." So, he told me just to wait, that he would be there in a minute. I went on back to the lobby and waited about five minutes for the movie to finish—he liked cowboy movies—then he came out and I got him back down to the auditorium. After that the Colonel called me in and said that he needed a responsible person to follow Elvis around and that I was it.

So right away I took a pay cut because I made more money selling pictures and programs than I did as a bodyguard. That started my having to be with Elvis constantly, almost twenty-four hours a day. Elvis was always very reluctant about being on time, didn't want to get there and if you pushed him he would slow up more. Elvis was a nice guy but he still had too much teenage stuff in him. That is why they needed me.

Elvis went into the service around 1958 or somewhere along then and I stayed over here. They wanted me to go overseas with him but I said no, I was staying here with my family. Then of course, I met him at Fort Dix when he got out and stayed with him through 1973. I left him in Mobile, Alabama, in 1973. I told the Colonel that I'd had enough of the road, what with baseball and Elvis. I was at every Elvis Presley concert from 1956 through 1973 and that is a lot of traveling. I was in charge of every security situation at the auditoriums, although over the years I pulled back away from the bodyguard bit.

I was the only bodyguard that Elvis had to start with. I used to have to guard his house on Audubon Drive in Memphis—front, back, sides, all at one time. Anyway, here comes Joe Esposito, who he had met in the service, and Joe started taking over some of my responsibilities. I kind of had to break him in. Then here come Red West and here come Sonny and Charlie and all the rest of them. That relieved me. It tickled me to death that I didn't have to follow him around at night anymore. But, I was still in charge of his security as far as transportation from city to city, hotel to auditorium, and auditorium back to the hotel and so forth. I still had quite a bit of responsibility, and after I got all that done I was the Colonel's right-hand man. It was worse working for him. I guess he was tougher on me than anyone because his wife was my older sister.

Did you know I was in a couple of Elvis's movies with him? I played in *G.I. Blues* and *Loving You*. They were just little background roles with no speaking. In *G.I. Blues* we had this one community sing-along scene that we had to keep reshooting because every time Elvis turned around and saw me back there singing along he would break down laughing. It was all real fun. I did it mainly for my kids to enjoy. I talk about all this in a book I wrote about Elvis. A book I wrote about Elvis but can't get published. The problem is that I tell the truth in it. The publishers all said that there wasn't enough sensationalism in it. Maybe I will try again someday. It has been a while since the last time.

Later on after leaving Elvis, I went to work for Brunswick Billiards. I was the service manager for the state of Florida. I always liked to work on pool tables doing repairs. If you have ever seen the pool table up at Graceland then you've seen some of my work. I put the cloth on it. After that, I stopped working for them and went to work for myself with my own pool table service and that is where I retired from. Oh, I also used to spend some time playing clown for children's parties. I'd get all dressed up and do tricks and that kind of thing. I called myself "Bobo the Hobo" and I used to have a ball with it.

Well, after my wife retired from the Florida State Fair Association we moved on up here to Blue Ridge, Georgia. I had visited my son up here and just loved it. I've got 12.2 acres on this hillside and when I found it I knew that it was the place for me. I mow 4 acres of it myself. It is a lot of work but the view out there is worth the effort.

I'll tell you, this business of baseball burns me up. Even though I am an ex-ballplayer, I am strictly for the owners and it is not because I am jealous of the money or anything. Let them make the money. But, let them be reasonable about it. They have so many more advantages today. When I played baseball, if a club signed you they owned you for the rest of your life or until they felt you weren't worth owning. Today players make in meal money per day what we made in a month. I think that today's ballplayers have just about overstepped their bounds.

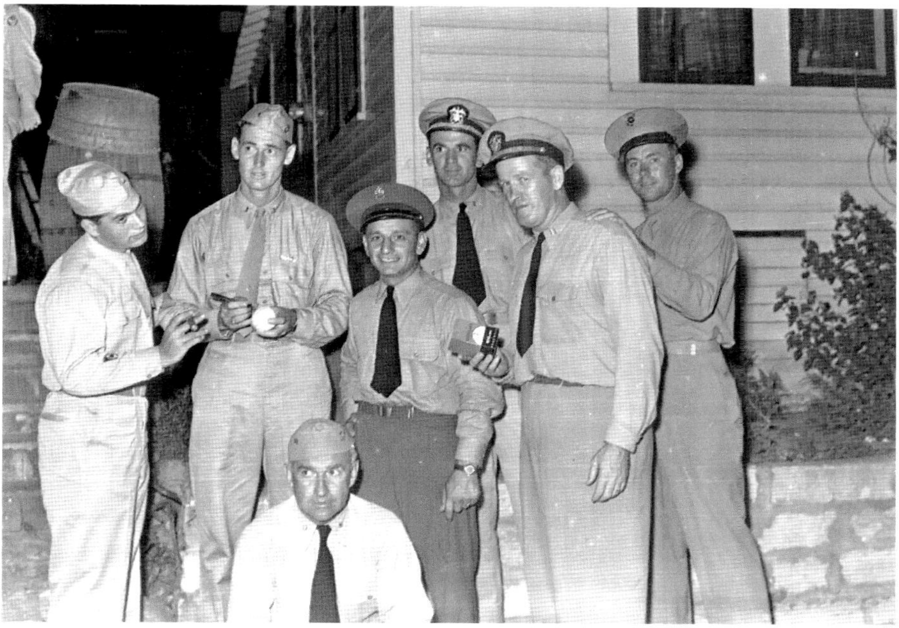

Ted Williams signing autographs during World War II. *Courtesy Florida State Archives.*

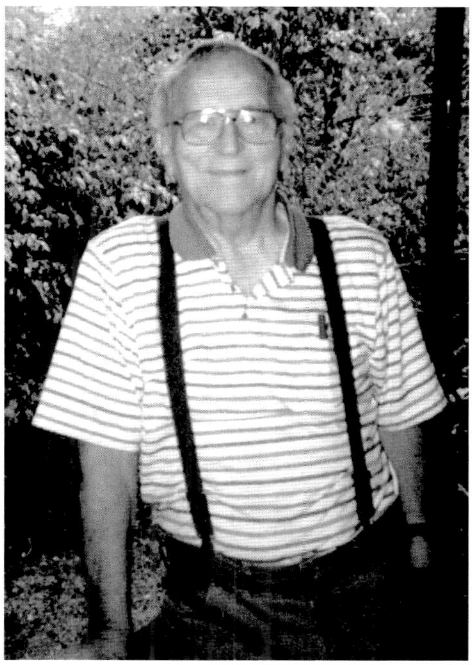

Bitsy Mott at home in Blue Ridge, Georgia, 1993. *Photo by author.*

I sure don't think that ballplayers today are any better than they were when I played. I am convinced that there are some ballplayers today that couldn't even make Class B ball in 1950. Baseball has just thinned out too much. There are so many chances now. Expansion has spread the talent too thin. I'd come home some nights after a loss and tell my wife that I would gladly give my salary today if we could have beaten that club. I like players that come to the park to play. Yeah, there are still plenty good ones out there but the talent has thinned.

My favorite all-time ballplayer is Ted Williams. No record would have stood if he hadn't lost so much time to the military while serving his country. He was the greatest player of all time, period. Did you know that if an umpire called a strike on Williams and Williams questioned the call, the umpire figured that Williams must be right? They had that much respect for his vision. Ted Williams had an eye out of this world. What a player he was.

Charlie Cuellar

Hell, he played in every city in the country.

—Benny Fernandez, *Tampa Tribune*, January 19, 1994

Charlie Cuellar was born in Ybor City, Tampa, Florida, to Cuban parents who had traveled to Ybor City for the cigar trade. Cuellar, "Marco Polo of the minors," posted in excess of two hundred professional victories in stops at Minneapolis, Reidsville, Decatur and Tampa, among others, yet his big-league career, two games with the Chicago White Sox, pulled up lame. One of the highlights of Cuellar's career came while pitching for the Tampa Smokers of the Florida International League against the vaunted Havana Cubans. Cuellar, who himself had pitched for Almendarés in the Cuban league, chucked a no-hitter in front of a packed Tampa house of boisterous cigar makers.

I was born here in Tampa, Ybor City, and this is where I grew up. My parents, John and Regla Cuellar, were from Cuba. During the 1890s, my daddy came over, like so many others, to work in the cigar factories and when he found a job my mother came too. I'm not positive but I think that my grandparents immigrated to Cuba from Spain, most of them had. Both of my parents went to work in the cigar factories. My daddy was a cigar maker and my mother was what they called a stripper. She stripped the vein from the tobacco leaf. They worked there all their lives but they didn't make any money, maybe five or six dollars a week.

I went to Ybor City Elementary School and George Washington Junior High. I began playing ball when I was ten years old. I loved to pitch and I did so every chance I could. I had a good curveball and I got better and better. We used to play at the city park in West Tampa and for the American Legion team there. When I played on that legion

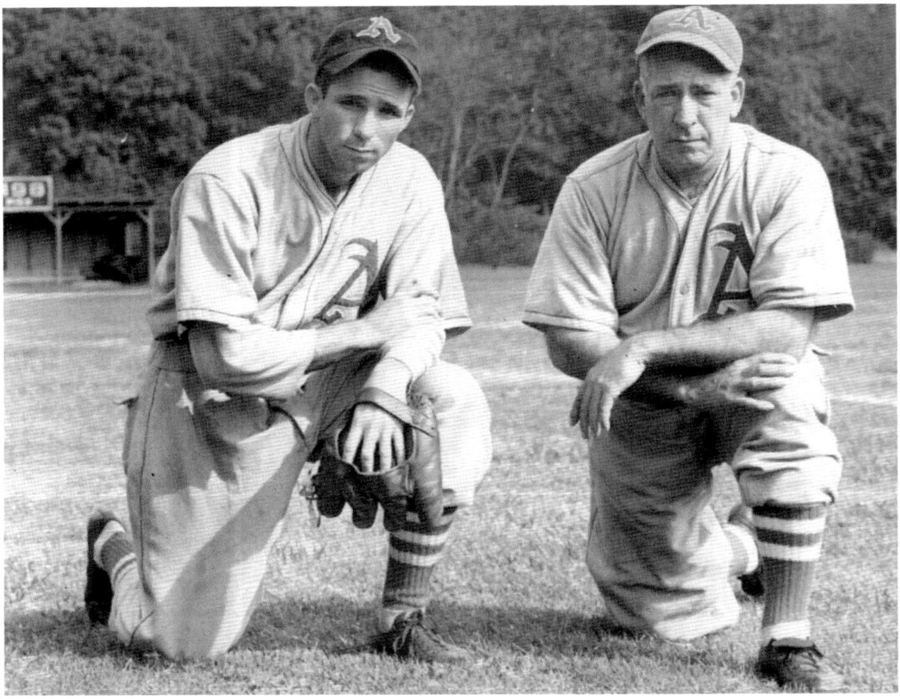

Charlie Cuellar and Adolfo Luque in Cuba with the Almendarés Alacranes, 1940. "He [Luque] was a son of a bitch to play for." *Courtesy National Baseball Library, Cooperstown, New York.*

team, we missed winning the National American Legion tournament by one game. We got all the way to the finals and we lost to Gastonia, North Carolina. That was in 1934. After that I graduated from junior high and by the next year I was playing professional baseball. There weren't too many from around here then playing professional ball.

The way I was signed was that Cincinnati used to train here in Tampa and in 1935 I was invited to come and train with them. Charlie Dressen was the manager of the team and he kind of liked me so he sent me to the Minneapolis Millers in Deland, Florida, a farm club. The Minneapolis team liked me so they sent me to Decatur, Illinois, in the Class D Three-I League and that's how I began my professional baseball career. My parents didn't mind my leaving home to play ball. My daddy was a great baseball fan. He died in 1943, so I hadn't played too much before he passed on.

There were a lot of good ballplayers there in Decatur that I got to play with. Frank McCormick, who later played with Cincinnati, was a hell of a good first baseman. Birdie Tebbets, a future manager in the big leagues, was the catcher. We had a good

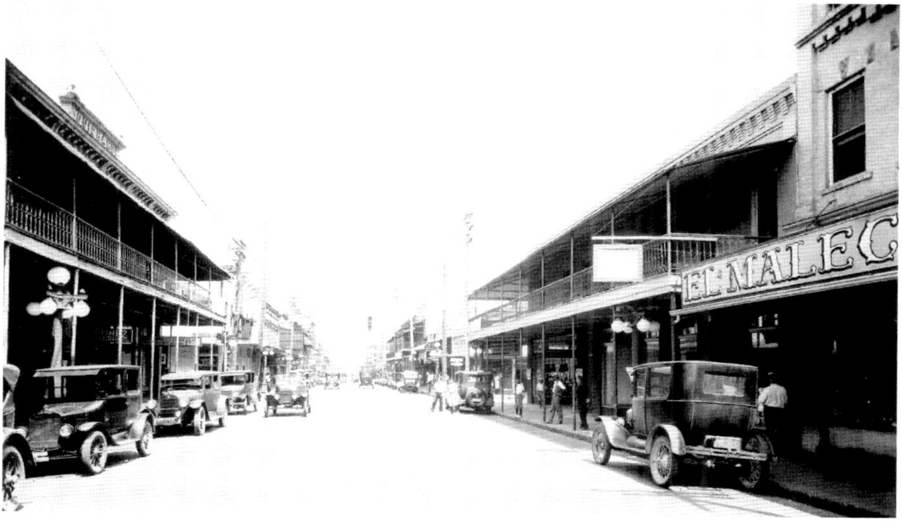

View down Seventh Avenue from Sixteenth Street, Ybor City, 1921. *Courtesy Florida State Archives.*

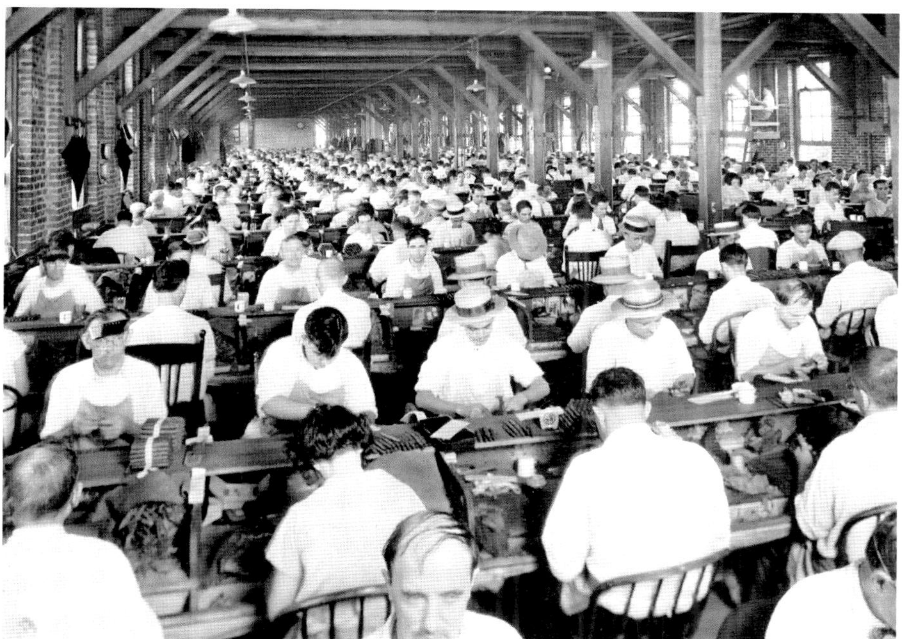

Ybor City cigar workers. *Courtesy Florida State Archives.*

team. The next two years I played in Marshall, Texas, and won thirteen ballgames as a pitcher. After that, 1938, I was sold to Pensacola of the Southeastern League and won two games before being sold again to Palestine in the East Texas League. In Palestine I won another fourteen games or so.

The next season, 1939, I was sold to Reidsville in the Bi-State League, and I won seventeen games. At Reidsville, I began to feel like I was really taking off. That off-season I played my first winter baseball in Cuba. I played for a club by the name of Almendarés. Cuba had a hell of a league. It was just as strong as any Double- or Triple-A league that I ever played in. There were many players there that went on to the Majors. Adolfo Luque was one of my managers in Cuba. They used to call Luque the "Havana Perfecto." They named him that after the best cigars in Cuba, since he was the best to have come out of there. He had always been a hell of a pitcher but what a temper! He was a son of a bitch to play for. Luque would fight anybody, but he could pitch. He was a good manager but that temper kept him from getting along too well with the players. Sal Maglie played in Cuba too. Luque had a lot to do with his success, working with him both in Cuba and Mexico. Luque taught him to take control while he was on the mound and not to give in to the batter.

I split the next season between Reidsville and Leakesville in the same league. That spring I was given a tryout with the Brooklyn Dodgers based on my winter in Cuba. Things didn't work out though. Anyway, in 1940 I won seventeen games and I followed that with sixteen wins in 1941. During one stretch in this period I pitched forty games without any relief. Do you think that anyone could do that today? Pitchers today are just not strong enough. There is no reason why a pitcher can't throw nine innings if he is in shape. How many times do you see a really good starter go seven or eight innings, look sharp, and then the big strong reliever comes in and ruins the game? It happens all the time. The starter should go the distance and then he wouldn't have to worry about it. I prefer to see a pitcher stay in there.

Yeah, I had a lot of good records in the minor leagues. There was a year there, one of my best, 1942, when I won twenty-two games and lost six for Leakesville. I struck out over 200 [208] and had an earned run average of 1.56, I think. I did so well that season that Leakesville sold me to Portsmouth, Virginia, in the Piedmont League. After I had won just four games for Portsmouth, I was sold to Tyler, Texas, but then Tyler went to hell; they disbanded. So I came back to Tampa for the rest of the year and worked in the shipyards. While I was here in Tampa, I kept busy playing for a shipyard team and for the Cuban club in the Inter-Social League.

Benny Fernandez, a future teammate of mine on the Tampa Smokers, was on that Cuban club team. His brother Manuel, who also played for the Smokers, caught for

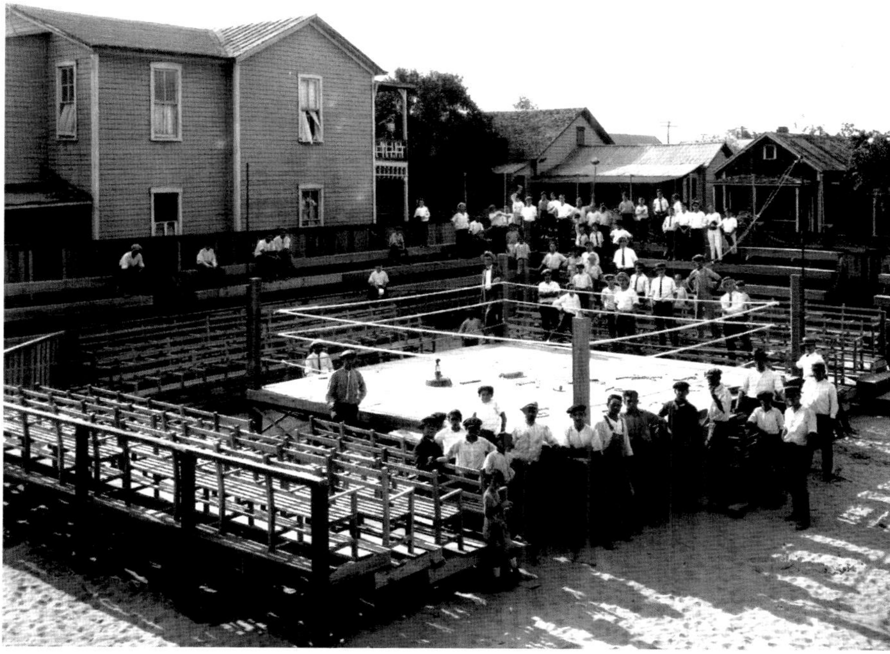

Boxing at El Círculo Cubano, the Cuban club in Ybor City, 1924. *Courtesy Florida State Archives.*

Centro Asturiano, a rival club. Manuel joined the navy before the end of the season and went into the war.

In Tampa, during the war, there were some other good teams that were made up of military players from Drew Field. I think Hank Greenberg played here then and some other big leaguers as well. They all played in the Inter-Social League.

I returned to organized baseball the next season with Nashville of the Southern Association. Larry Gilbert was the manager there, a really nice man. I think that I won seventeen and lost six with the Vols. I was unable to pitch the last month of the season on account of an arm injury. My arm would tighten up and cause me a great deal of pain. From then on, every time I pitched I'd have to spend a lot of time warming up. This is what hurt me later on in the big leagues. If I hadn't hurt my arm in Nashville I would have won a lot more games. I tried to have it worked on. I used to go to this doctor in Miami and he would pull on it and stretch it and he could make it feel good. But once I pitched again it would get tight on me.

From Nashville I went to Los Angeles of the Pacific Coast League, 1945, and won thirteen games and I think I lost seventeen. It was a bad year; the team lost a hundred ballgames. I decided the next season that I'd had enough of Los Angeles and their losing so I refused to report. They said that if I could make a deal for myself to go ahead. Well, I had always wanted to play at home so I arranged a deal between Los Angeles and Tampa, in the Florida International League, and I joined the Smokers in May 1946. I won fifteen games for them that season.

That was a big mistake of mine, staying here with the Smokers, I should have gone back. The Pacific Coast League was a higher classification league and I would have been better off staying there. But baseball was like a chain gang then. Once you signed a contract you were obligated to that team for as long as you played ball and for whatever pay they gave you, unless they released you. The players didn't have the upper hand then like they do now. So when I had the chance to go home and play I took it.

In 1947 I won another fifteen games for the Smokers. Tony Cuccinello, Al Lopez's old teammate, was the manager in Tampa. Benny and Manuel Fernandez, Bitsy Mott, Citayo Gonzalez, Lamar Murphy, Gene Elliott, Dick Dendinger, Joe Benedito, Marcelo Masaeda were all on that team. It was a good team. On July 23 of that season I pitched against the Havana Cubans in the most exciting game I can remember. Many of the guys on my team, except for maybe Mott, Murphy, Elliott and Dendinger, were local Cubans like me, so you can imagine that it was a big deal playing against Havana. That day, as always when Havana came to play in Tampa, the stands at Plant Field were packed. Earlier in the season Havana had no-hit us and won, but this time we turned it around. I pitched eight strikeouts and walked only one. Two others reached base on errors but I still got the no-hit shutout and we won 5–0. With the big crowds that we drew playing Havana, the no-hitter meant a lot to everybody. The tension in that game was so great. Any time Havana came to Tampa, the town would be in an uproar because so many Cuban people here rooted for Havana. When I pitched the no-hitter, the place went wild. There were seat cushions all over the field. The people were going bananas. It really was such a big rivalry. The Tampa fans later rewarded me with a special day and the team gave me an engraved watch for the victory. It was quite a feeling. In 1948 I won another seventeen games for the Smokers.

I saw Bitsy Mott not all that long ago. Bitsy is living up in Georgia now and a couple of the guys I played with on the Smokers, Benny Fernandez and Lamar Murphy, went with me to see him. Benny has a place in North Carolina where we had gone and on the way back we stopped off in Georgia to visit Bitsy. Lamar Murphy was a hell of a hitter. I don't think he made it to the big leagues because they didn't like his arm but he was a hell of a hitter. The Smokers had a lot of local Tampa guys playing for them. Benny Fernandez was another guy who could hit the hell out of the ball. He was a great first baseman too. Manuel Fernandez couldn't hit as well as his brother but he was a damn good catcher. Manuel is the one who caught me when I pitched the no-hitter against Havana. I think that the only thing that kept Benny Fernandez out of the big leagues is that he didn't care to go anywhere. He loved it here. Benny ended up working thirty-something years for the State Hotel and Restaurant Commission and still lives here in Tampa.

The following season, 1949, in a surprise deal, I was sold to the Lakeland Pilots as a manager. When I came to Lakeland from Tampa, I pitched four games against the Smokers and beat them all four times. It was with Lakeland that I won my 200th minor league game. It took me three tries after I had won the 199th to get the next one. On the first try I pitched a two-hitter against Miami and lost, then next I pitched a five-hitter against the same club at Miami Beach and lost, then I threw another five-hitter against Miami and lost again. Finally on the fourth try I made it. We beat St. Petersburg.

When I was managing at Lakeland, 1950, I was sold to the Chicago White Sox. I could have gone to the Washington Senators or the White Sox but I picked Chicago and made a big mistake. Back then most of the Cuban players that went to the big leagues went to the Senators and did real good. I should have gone there too but I didn't. Do you know what it is in this business for a guy like me to win two hundred games before ever getting to the big leagues? That was unbelievable! Believe me, I still don't know what took them so long because I was a winner wherever I went.

There was a scout down here—I can't remember his name—that kind of liked me and he thought that I could pitch in the big leagues. I would have too if they hadn't put me as a relief pitcher. I had always been a starter and they put me in there as a reliever and I just wasn't a relief pitcher. I could never pitch in relief. Plus, remember when I was in Nashville I hurt my arm and I couldn't pitch every other day or always be getting up to throw in the bullpen. If I could pitch every third or fourth day I would give you a good game. I don't think I relieved five times in my life and I had a 253–130 lifetime record. But once I warmed up I had to go ahead and pitch. I couldn't sit back down and wait just because the pitcher that was in there had settled down. My arm couldn't take the ups and downs of the bullpen. It was hard for me to go through that and frustrating too. I couldn't do it. I appeared in two games for Chicago and got shelled. I guess it was my tough luck not to make it in the big leagues, because everywhere else I went I was a winner.

To show you what I am talking about, I left Chicago and went to Memphis in the Southern Association and won nine games just like that—all as a starter. While I was in Memphis I had a tussle with Luke Appling, the manager, over this same thing. One game I pitched for Memphis was a shutout and after that we went to New Orleans. While in New Orleans, Appling wanted me to pitch some batting practice and I told him that I couldn't do it because my arm was too sore. Well, he says that if you're going to pitch for me you're going to have to pitch batting practice and I told him that I couldn't do it. Well, I went up there and tried because he made me, but I could hardly throw the ball. Finally I told him that if he wanted me to stay with Memphis then he would have to let me get my rest. I told him that if he pitched me every three or four days I would give him a hell of a ballgame but otherwise I couldn't do it. Appling, I guess he didn't care, stuck to it and told me that anybody who pitches for him had to pitch batting practice. So I said fine, I wasn't pitching for him. I came back here to the Florida International League and pitched for the St. Petersburg Saints. At St. Petersburg I won some more games and never had another losing season after that.

Not too many people stay in the minor leagues as long as I did. I was the "Marco Polo of the minor leagues." I played everywhere; won 253 games against 130 losses. That is not counting all of the ball that I played during the winters in Cuba. At every level I won a lot more than I lost. Nobody could ever do what I did again. Who stays in the minors long enough to put up numbers like that today? And I pitched complete games 97 percent of the time. But the arm trouble eventually ran me out after 1955.

You know, a lot of the fans used to think that I won so many games because I threw spitballs. That was a lot of shit! I just had a habit of wetting my pitching hand when I was out on the mound. But then I would dry it by wiping it on my uniform and you can see from the old pictures, the smudge spot where I wiped it. The reason I used to do this was because when you use the rosin bag sometimes your hands would get kind of smooth. So I would lick my fingers to give me a better grip on the ball. But every time I went to my mouth, I wiped off my hand. That is why my jerseys have that dark spot in those pictures. I never threw a spitball. But you know, if I was going to throw a spitter I could have learned it from Burleigh Grimes, the last great spitball pitcher. I played with him for a while in Minneapolis in 1935 after he left the big leagues. Grimes was only a reliever for us but he was something else. I imagine that Burleigh could have taught me to throw a good one.

My last baseball game was in Tallahassee. I went there to manage the club, which was owned by the Pirates and played its ball at the old Centennial Field. Earlier, I had finished as a full-time player in Keokuk, Iowa. Although I was sent to Tallahassee to manage, I thought that I might help out by pitching a little if the team needed me to. I was only there two days when the league went under. Oh well, that was enough for me.

After I retired from playing ball I started doing a little house painting. It was all that I knew how to do. I only had a junior high school education and since I was just thirty-five, I had to work at something. I had learned on my own to do some woodwork, and I started building bars or whatever people wanted and as time went on word spread and I got more woodworking jobs than painting. After that I started

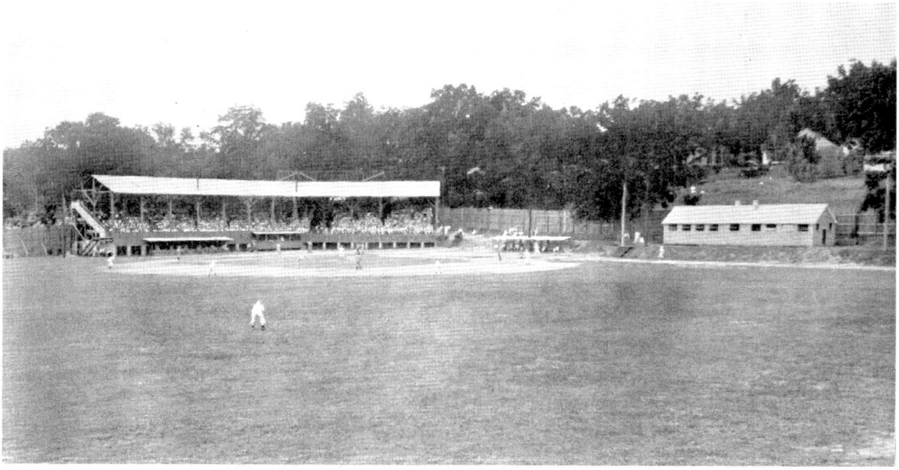

Marco Polo's final stop, Centennial Field, Tallahassee, Florida. *Courtesy Florida State Archives.*

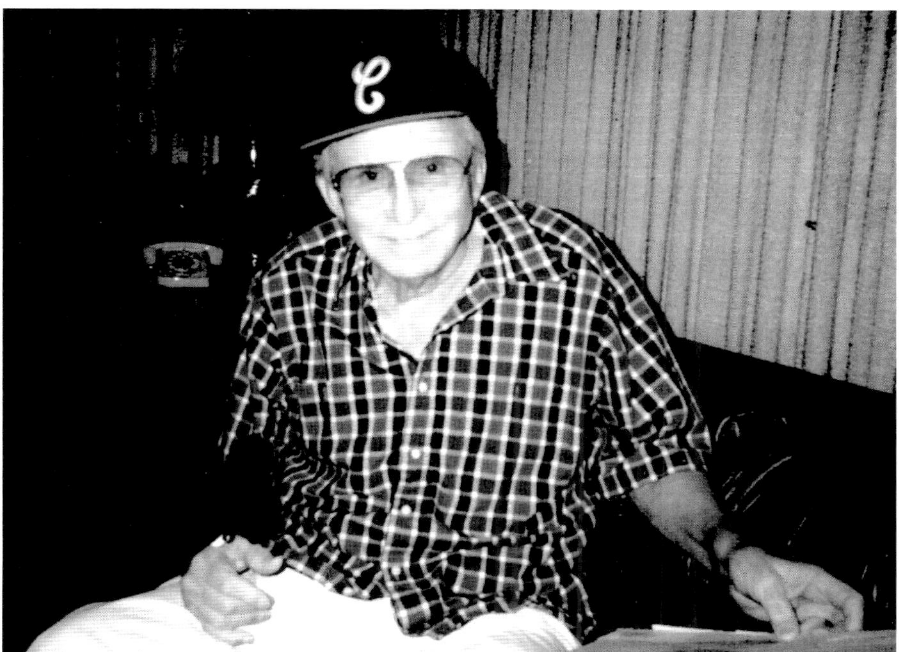

Charlie Cuellar at home in Tampa, Florida, 1993. *Photo by author.*

to do nothing but woodwork. My reputation for good work got around and I began remodeling penthouses, beach condominiums and offices as well as houses. I can go into a house and right away know what I'm going to do and how it's going to look. I've been lucky and very busy doing a lot of nice homes. Some of the work that I've done has been featured in *Tampa Bay Southern Homes* and *Tampa Bay Homes* magazines.

Tampa has really gotten big over the years, but I like it here. We are in a nice neighborhood, close to Dale Mabry Avenue, and that has everything on it. Of course, in the last five years more people have gone to the Majors from here than at any other time. When I went to the Majors in 1950, no one had gone from here except Al Lopez, Manuel Onis and Bitsy Mott. But I don't think Bitsy was born here in Tampa. I once played somewhere with Max Macon, he was another guy from Florida. There just weren't many of us back then.

I met my wife Dahlia at a tea dance at the Centro Español Club here in Tampa. We corresponded while I was playing baseball around the country and were eventually married. We have been married thirty-two years. Dahlia was always a good fan; she enjoyed my playing. She worked at Tampa Electric for thirty-eight years until she retired in 1990. We are usually here around the house. Until recently you would probably find me out back doing something in the workshop. Not so much anymore. We've both been very lucky.

Index

A

Allen, Johnny 89
Alvarez, Cesare 22
Antonelli, John 101
Apalachicola, FL 12, 63, 67, 69, 70
Aparicio, Luis 23, 39
Appalachian League 83, 84
Appling, Luke 117, 118
Ashburn, Richie 69, 90, 91
Atlanta Crackers 23, 26, 27

B

Baker, Del 65
Barrett, Frank 12, 72, 73, 79
Barry, Jack 98
Bauer, Hank 77
Beradino, Johnny 65
Berres, Ray 31, 32
Bigelow, Elliot 49, 50
Bi-State League 114
Blackwell, Ewell 77
Bloodworth, Jimmy 11, 12, 63, 64, 71, 75, 91
Boone, Bob 33
Boone, Ike 22
Boston Braves 4, 22, 29, 30, 31, 33, 59, 60, 77, 78, 80
Boston Red Sox 47, 48, 50, 51, 78
Bradenton Field 96
Branca, Ralph 81
Brandt, Ed 59, 60
Braves Field 30, 33
Brecheen, Harry 76
Brooklyn Dodgers 23, 25, 26, 27, 28, 29, 31, 54, 56, 57, 60, 61, 84, 87, 88, 89, 90, 97
Robins 26, 34, 67, 90, 114

C

Cain, John 74
Campanella, Roy 67
Cantwell, Ben 25

Centennial Field (Tallahassee) 118
Centro Asturiano 98
Centro Español Club 105, 120
Chapman, Ben 85, 100, 101, 102, 105, 106
Chicago White Sox 16, 111, 117
Cincinnati Reds 23, 31, 32, 33, 34, 43, 46, 63, 65, 69, 75, 81, 103, 112
Cleveland Indians 16, 33, 37, 38, 46
Cobb, Ty 11, 41
Cochrane. Mickey 32, 52
Colavito, Rocky 68
Columbus Redbirds 76
Covington, Chet 103
Cronin, Joe 52, 78
Crosetti, Frank 64
Cuban Stars (Tampa) 56
Cuccinello, Tony 29, 33, 34, 79, 103, 104, 116
Cuellar, Charlie 11, 12, 98, 102, 103, 111, 112, 119

D

Damon, Johnny 9
Daniels, Fred 98, 101
Dark, Alvin 78, 88
Dawson, Andre 9
Dean, Dizzy 25, 51
Detroit Tigers 25, 35, 63, 64, 65, 66, 67, 68, 75
Dickey, Bill 32, 52, 64
DiMaggio, Joe 35, 64
DiMaggio, Vince 35, 100
Dinges, Vance 98, 101
Doby, Larry 24, 90
Doer, Bobby 65
Dressen, Charlie 112
Duren, Ryne 42, 43
Durocher, Leo 52, 87, 88, 90, 91
Dyer, Eddie 75

E

Earnshaw, George 51
East Texas League 114
Ebbets Field 57
Ennis, Del 91
Everett, Carl 9

F

Feller, Bob 25, 36, 38, 40, 66, 71
Fenway Park 78
Fernandez, Benny 103, 114, 116
Fernandez, Manuel 98, 114, 116
Ferrell, Rick 64
Ferrell, Wes 64
Florida International League 97, 102, 111, 116, 118
Florida State League 97, 103
Fournier, Jacques 22
Fox, Nelson 39
Foxx, Jimmy 52, 100

G

Garagiola, Joe 77
Garcia, Mike 38, 40
Garrison, Ford 99
Garvey, Steve 9
Gaston, Milt 52
Gehringer, Charlie 25, 47, 52, 64, 65
Georgia-Florida League 57, 97
Gonzalez, Luis 9
Gonzalez, Mike 24
Gooden, Doc 9
Gordon, Joe 39, 65

Greenberg, Hank 38, 68, 69, 115
Grimes, Burleigh 26, 118
Grove, Robert Moses 25, 51, 65

H

Hansen, Andy 11, 12, 13, 81, 82, 94
Harris, Bucky 21, 65
Hartnett, Gabby 32, 33, 84, 89
Havana Cubans 102
Hegan, Jim 33, 38, 41
Henline, Butch 97
Herman, Babe 28, 29
Houtteman, Art 38, 40

I

Inter-Social League (Tampa) 97, 114, 115
Irvin, Monte 41, 89, 90, 91

J

Jacksonville Tars 10, 23, 25, 26, 57, 74, 83
Johnson, Walter 20, 21, 22, 25, 51

K

Keesler Field (Keesler Air Force Base) 86
Kiner, Ralph 69
Kluszewski, Ted 42, 69

L

Lake Worth, FL 81
Landis, Jim 42
LaRussa, Tony 9, 43, 46
Lazzeri, Tony 64
Lemon, Bob 36, 38, 40
Leonard, Dutch 68
Lewis, Duffy 48
Lloyd, John Henry 9, 10
Lockman, Whitey 84, 88
Lollar, Sherm 42
Lombardi, Ernie 34, 89
Lopez, Al 4, 10, 11, 12, 16, 17, 18, 20, 22, 27, 31, 37, 40, 42, 43, 54, 56, 57, 63, 67, 72, 78, 103, 116, 120
Luque, Adolfo 23, 112, 114

M

Mack, Connie 39, 52, 68, 98
Mack, George 83
Macon Peaches 23
Magerkurth, George L. 59
Maglie, Sal 88, 114
Martin, Pepper 76, 88, 95
Martinez, Tino 9
Mays, Carl 50
Mays, Willie 40
McGraw, John 27, 29, 85
McKechnie, Bill 28, 31, 46
McLaurin, Ralph 11
McRae, Hal 9
Mid-Atlantic League 60
Miller, Eddie 81
Mize, Johnny 87, 88, 94
Mott, Elisha Matthew "Bitsy" 11, 13, 95, 96, 99, 101, 109, 116, 120
Mungo, Van Lingle 29, 34, 89
Murphy, Lamar 116

N

Nance, Doc 19
Newcombe, Don 67
Newhouser, Hal 38, 66, 67

New York Giants 23, 27, 28, 40, 69, 81, 82, 84, 86, 87, 88, 89, 90, 100
New York Yankees 16, 40, 50, 57, 65

O

Onis, Manuel 11, 12, 54, 61, 120
Orange Belt League 96
Ott, Mel 84, 85, 86, 87, 88, 89, 90, 100

P

Pacific Coast League 115
Palatka Azaleas 103, 105
Parker, Tom 106
Pensacola, FL 47
Pensacola Flyers 53
Phelps, Babe 57
Philadelphia Phillies 63, 81, 90, 91, 96, 100, 103
Piedmont League 114
Piniella, Lou 9, 43, 46
Piniella, Lou, Sr. 98
Pittsburgh Pirates 92
Plant Field 102, 116
Platt, Whitey 76
Polo Grounds 41, 84, 88
Porter, Ned 69, 70
Presley, Elvis 13, 95, 106, 107, 108

R

Rhodes, Dusty 40
Richbourg, Lance 10
Rickey, Branch 75, 92, 93
Rizzuto, Phil 77
Roberts, Robin 69, 91
Robinson, Wilbert 26, 27, 28, 46
Rodolfo, Arias 43
Rodriguez, Alex 9
Roe, Preacher 77
Rosen, Al 36
Rucker, Nap 25
Ruffing, Red 50
Ruth, George Herman 10, 50, 52, 58, 64, 106
Ryan, Jack 48

S

Sain, Johnny 78
Sawyer, Eddie 66
Scarritt, Russ 11, 12, 47
Score, Herb 37, 38, 68
Seminick, Andy 91, 103
Sewell, Rip 35
Sheffield, Gary 9
Simmons, Al 68
Simmons, Curt 91
Sisler, Dick 91
Slaughter, Enos 75
Smith, Mayo 81
Snider, Duke 67
Southeastern League 75, 114
Southern Association 93
South Atlantic League 23, 48, 75
Spahn, Warren 78
St. Leo College 72, 80
St. Louis Cardinals 11, 32, 38, 43, 46, 65, 72, 73, 74, 75, 76, 86, 95
St. Petersburg Saints 118
Stanky, Eddie 88
Stengel, Casey 30, 31, 40, 46, 54, 57

T

Tampa, FL 4, 45, 54, 55, 100, 102, 111, 119
Tampa Baseball School 101, 104

Tampa Smokers 18, 19, 24, 97, 102, 104, 111, 114, 116
Taylor, Zach 77
Tebbetts, Birdie 37
Terry, Bill 29, 69
Tewksbury, Bob 80
Texas League 76
Thompson, Hank 89
Thomson, Bobby 81, 90
Travis, Cecil 68
Traynor, Pie 26
Triplett, Coaker 75, 101
Trout, Dizzy 66

V

Vance, Dazzy 25, 26, 28
Vander Meer, Johnny 77
Vaughan, Arky 33
Virginia League 19
Voiselle, Bill 86

W

Wagner, Honus 10
Walters, Bucky 65
Wasdell, Jimmy 101
Washington Senators 20, 21, 23, 63, 64
Wertz, Vic 38, 39, 40, 41
Wheat, Zach 25
Williams, Ted 33, 66, 68, 109, 110
Wright, Glen 26
Wynn, Early 36, 38

Y

Yankee Stadium 52, 64
Ybor City, FL 10, 12, 17, 18, 46, 54, 55, 56, 61, 97, 106, 111, 113, 115

About the Author

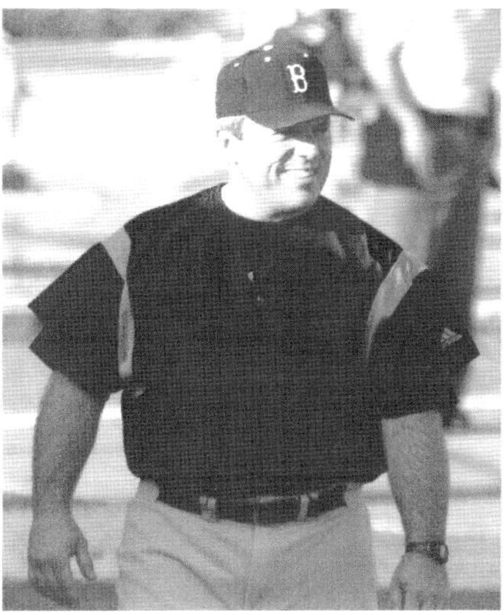

Wes Singletary, a native of Tampa, holds a doctorate in United States History from Florida State University, where he also taught for two years. He is currently Executive Director for the Discovery of Florida Quincentennial Commission, Florida Department of State, mapping a statewide celebration of Florida's Quincentennial in 2013. Wes has taught history at the Brookwood School in Thomasville, Georgia, and has served as an adjunct history professor at Tallahassee Community College since 1993. He further serves as a reader for the College Board in its Advanced Placement History program, is a Board member for the Leon County Schools Foundation, and is the recipient of a Gilder-Lehrman Institute of American History fellowship. While at Brookwood, Wes helped coach the Warriors baseball team to consecutive GISA Class 2A Georgia State Baseball Championships.

Wes Singletary is also the author of *Al Lopez: The Life of Baseball's El Senor* and is presently working on a biography of John Henry "Pop" Lloyd, a baseball hall-of-famer from the Negro Leagues; both are Florida natives. He is married to the former Toni Zarate and they have two children, Patricia and Nelson. They live in Tallahassee, Florida.